MATHEMAT

for

AQA GCSE (Modular)

STUDENT SUPPORT BOOK

Foundation Tier

Tony Banks and David Alcorn

CPL

Causeway Press Limited

Published by Causeway Press Ltd
P.O. Box 13, Ormskirk, Lancashire L39 5HP

First published 2003

© Tony Banks and David Alcorn

British Library Cataloguing-in-Publication Data.
A catalogue record for this book is available from the British Library.

ISBN 1-902796-60-8

Acknowledgements
Past exam questions, provided by the *Assessment and Qualifications Alliance*, are denoted by the letters AQA. The answers to all questions are entirely the responsibility of the authors/publisher and have neither been provided nor approved by AQA.

Every effort has been made to locate the copyright owners of material used in this book. Any omissions brought to the notice of the publisher are regretted and will be credited in subsequent printings.

Page design
Billy Johnson

Reader
Anne Alcock

Artwork
David Alcorn

Cover design
Waring-Collins Partnership

Typesetting by Billy Johnson, San Francisco, California, USA

Printed and bound by Scotprint, Haddington, Scotland

preface

This book provides detailed revision notes, worked examples and examination questions to support students in their preparation for AQA GCSE Mathematics (Modular) at the Foundation Tier of Entry.

The book has been designed so that it can be used in conjunction with the companion book *Mathematics for AQA GCSE (Modular) - Foundation Tier* or as a stand-alone revision book for self study and provides full coverage of AQA Specification B (Modular).

In preparing the text, full account has been made of the requirements for students to be able to use and apply mathematics in written examination papers and be able to solve problems in mathematics both with and without a calculator.

The detailed revision notes, worked examples and examination questions have been organised into 34 self-contained sections which meet the requirements of the National Curriculum and provide efficient coverage of the specifications for Modules 1, 3 and 5. Modules 2 and 4 are coursework tasks.

Module 1   Sections   1 - 6
Module 3   Sections   7 - 16
Module 5   Sections 17 - 34

At the end of Module 1 and Module 3 there is an examination questions section with a compilation of exam and exam-style questions, organised for non-calculator and calculator practice, in preparation for the exams.

In Module 5 a section review is provided at the end of Sections 17 - 24 (Number and Algebra) and another at the end of Sections 25 - 34 (Shape, Space and Measures) to give further opportunities to consolidate skills. At the end of the module there is a further compilation of exam and exam-style questions, organised for non-calculator and calculator practice, in preparation for the exams.

contents

Module 1

Sections 1 - 6

Module 3

Sections 7 - 16

Module 5

What you need to know

- **Primary data** is data collected by an individual or organisation to use for a particular purpose. Primary data is obtained from experiments, investigations, surveys and by using questionnaires.

- **Secondary data** is data which is already available or has been collected by someone else for a different purpose. Sources of secondary data include the Annual Abstract of Statistics, Social Trends and the Internet.

- **Qualitative** data – Data which can only be described in words.

- **Quantitative** data – Data that has a numerical value. Quantitative data is either **discrete** or **continuous**. **Discrete** data can only take certain values. **Continuous** data has no exact value and is measurable.

- **Data Collection Sheets** – Used to record data during a survey.

- **Tally** – A way of recording each item of data on a data collection sheet.
    A group of five is recorded as ⅠⅠⅠⅠ.

- **Frequency Table** – A way of collating the information recorded on a data collection sheet.

- **Grouped Frequency Table** – Used for continuous data or for discrete data when a lot of data has to be recorded.

- **Database** – A collection of data.

- **Class Interval** – The width of the groups used in a grouped frequency distribution.

- **Questionnaire** – A set of questions used to collect data for a survey. Questionnaires should:
    (1) use simple language,
    (2) ask short questions which can be answered precisely,
    (3) provide tick boxes,
    (4) avoid open-ended questions,
    (5) avoid leading questions,
    (6) ask questions in a logical order.

- **Hypothesis** – A hypothesis is a statement which may or may not be true.

- When information is required about a large group of people it is not always possible to survey everyone and only a **sample** may be asked.
    The sample chosen should be large enough to make the results meaningful and representative of the whole group (population).

- **Two-way Tables** – A way of illustrating two features of a survey.

Exercise 1

1 The table shows information about pupils in the same class at a school.

Name	Gender	Month of birth	Day of birth
Corrin	F	June	Monday
Daniel	M	March	Thursday
Laila	F	May	Friday
Ria	F	March	Tuesday
Miles	M	April	Tuesday

(a) Who was born in May?
(b) Who was born on a Tuesday in March?
(c) Which of these pupils is most likely to be the youngest? Give a reason for your answer.

2 Tayfan is organising a skiing holiday to Italy for his friends.

They can go to Cervinia, Livigno or Tonale. He asks each of his friends which resort they would like to go to and records the answers in his notebook.

Show a better way of recording this information.

Cervinia	Cervinia	Livigno	Tonale
Tonale	Tonale	Livigno	Cervinia
Livigno	Cervinia	Tonale	Tonale
Cervinia	Livigno	Tonale	Livigno
Tonale	Cervinia	Livigno	Tonale
Livigno	Tonale	Cervinia	

3 Meeta is doing a survey about sport.
She asks the question, "Do you play football, rugby or hockey?"
(a) Give a reason why this is not a suitable question.
(b) Write a similar question which is suitable.

4 Pat is investigating how long students spend on homework each night.
The time, in minutes, taken by 30 students to do their homework on a Wednesday night is shown.

| 100 | 55 | 45 | 80 | 65 | 40 | 10 | 45 | 105 | 60 | 35 | 40 | 30 | 45 | 90 |
| 25 | 120 | 55 | 60 | 75 | 70 | 45 | 90 | 45 | 90 | 45 | 25 | 15 | 20 | 75 |

(a) Using equal class intervals, copy and complete the frequency table to show this data.

Time (t minutes)	Tally	Frequency
$0 \leqslant t < 30$		

(b) Which class interval has the highest frequency?

5 The table shows the results of a survey of 500 people.

A newspaper headline states:

Survey shows that more women can drive than men.

	Can drive	Cannot drive
Men	180	20
Women	240	60

Do the results of the survey support this headline?
Give a reason for your answer.

6 A mobile phone company wants to build a transmitter mast on land belonging to a school.
The company offers the school £50 000 for the land.
The local paper receives 20 letters objecting to the proposal and 5 letters in favour.
One of the paper's reporters writes an article in which he claims:

'Objectors outnumber those in favour by 4 to 1'

Give **two** reasons why the newspaper reporter's claim may **not** be correct.

AQA

7 The two-way table shows the number of credit cards and the number of store cards owned by each of 50 shoppers.

Number of store cards

		0	1	2	3
	0	3	2	1	0
Number of	1	5	4	3	1
credit cards	2	8	6	4	3
	3	4	3	2	1

(a) How many of the shoppers had two credit cards and one store card?
(b) How many of the shoppers had three credit cards?
(c) How many of the shoppers had exactly one card?
(d) How many of the shoppers had more credit cards than store cards?

AQA

Presentation of Data 1

What you need to know

- **Pictogram**. Symbols are used to represent information.
  Each symbol can represent one or more items of data.

- **Bar chart**. Used for data which can be counted.
  Often used to compare quantities of data in a distribution.
  The length of each bar represents frequency.
  The longest bar represents the **mode**.
  The difference between the largest and smallest variable
  is called the **range**.

  > Bars can be drawn
  > horizontally or vertically.
  > Bars are the same width and
  > there are gaps between bars.

- **Bar-line graph**. Instead of drawing bars, horizontal or vertical lines are drawn to show frequency.

  Eg 1 The graph shows the number of goals scored by a football team in 10 matches.

  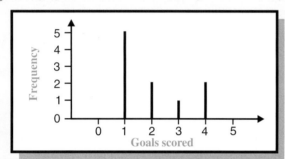

  (a) Which number of goals scored is the mode?
  (b) What is the range of the number of goals scored?

  (a) The tallest bar represents the mode. The mode is 1 goal.
  (b) The range is the difference between the largest and smallest number of goals scored.
  The range $= 4 - 1 = 3$

- **Pie chart**. Used for data which can be counted.
  Often used to compare proportions of data, usually with the total.
  The whole circle represents all the data.
  The size of each sector represents the frequency of data in that sector.
  The largest sector represents the **mode**.

  Eg 2 The pie chart shows the makes of 120 cars.
  (a) Which make of car is the mode?
  (b) How many of the cars are Ford?

  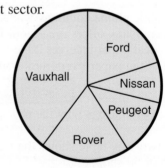

  (a) The sector representing Vauxhall is the largest.
  Therefore, Vauxhall is the mode.
  (b) The angle of the sector representing Ford is 72°.
  The number of Ford cars $= \dfrac{72}{360} \times 120 = 24$

- **Stem and leaf diagrams**. Used to represent data in its original form. Data is split into two parts.
  The part with the higher place value is the stem.   e.g.   15 = stem 1, leaf 5.
  A key is given to show the value of the data.   e.g.   3|4 means 3.4 etc.
  The data is shown in numerical order on the diagram.   e.g.   2|3 5 9 represents 23, 25, 29.

  Back to back stem and leaf diagrams can be used to compare two sets of data.

  Eg 3 The times, in seconds, taken by 10 students
  to complete a puzzle are shown.
  9 23 17 20 12 11 24 12 10 26
  Construct a stem and leaf diagram
  to represent this information.

			2|0 means 20 seconds		
0	9				
1	0	1	2	2	7
2	0	3	4	6	

1 Philip asks his friends what their favourite sport is.
The results are shown in the tally chart.

(a) How many friends chose football?

(b) How many friends did Philip ask?

(c) Draw a pictogram to show Philip's results.

Use the symbol ⊤ to represent 4 friends.

Sport	Tally
Football	ЖЖ ЖЖ II
Rugby	IIII
Racing	ЖЖ III
Other	ЖЖ ЖЖ

AQA

2 A sample of retired people was asked, "Which television channel do you watch the most?"
The table shows the results.

Television channel	BBC 1	BBC 2	ITV 1	Channel 4	Channel 5
Number of people	16	9	11	10	4

(a) Draw a bar chart to show these results.
(b) What percentage watched Channel 4 the most?

3 Causeway Hockey Club have a hockey team for men and a hockey team for women.
The bar chart shows the number of goals scored in matches played by these teams last season.

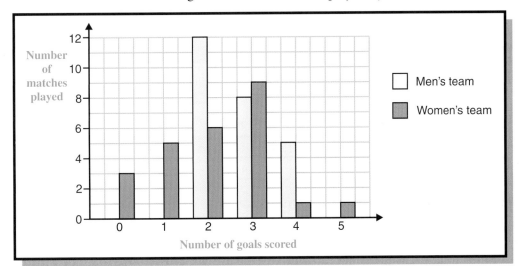

(a) How many matches did each team play?
(b) For the men's team, find the range and mode in the number of goals scored.
(c) Compare and comment on the goals scored by these teams last season.

4 The stem and leaf diagram shows the highest November temperature recorded in
12 European countries last year.

(a) How many countries are included?
(b) What is the maximum temperature recorded?
(c) Which temperature is the mode?
(d) What is the range of these temperatures?

```
                        0 | 7  means 7°C
0 | 7   9
1 | 0   3   4   4   4   7   8
2 | 0   1   2
```

5 The table shows the results of asking a group of children which pet they prefer.

Pet	Dog	Cat	Rabbit	Guinea pig
Number of children	8	5	7	4

Draw a clearly labelled pie chart to represent this information.

AQA

Averages and Range ●●●●●

What you need to know

● There are three types of **average**: the **mode**, the **median** and the **mean**.

Eg 1 The number of text messages received by 7 students on Saturday is shown.

$$2 \quad 4 \quad 3 \quad 4 \quad 4 \quad 3 \quad 2$$

Find   (a) the mode,   (b) the median,   (c) the mean,   (d) the range.

> The **mode** is the most common amount.
>
> The **median** is found by arranging the data in order of size and taking the middle amount (or the mean of the two middle amounts).
>
> The **mean** is found by dividing the total of all the data by the number of data values.
>
> The **range** is a measure of **spread**.
> Range = highest amount − lowest amount

(a) The mode is 4.

(b) 2   2   3   ③   4   4   4
     The median is 3.

(c) The mean $= \dfrac{2 + 4 + 3 + 4 + 4 + 3 + 2}{7}$

   $= \dfrac{22}{7} = 3.14\ldots$

   $= 3.1$, correct to 1 d.p.

(d) The range $= 4 - 2 = 2$

● To find the mean of a **frequency distribution** use: $\text{Mean} = \dfrac{\text{Total of all amounts}}{\text{Number of amounts}}$

Eg 2 The table shows the number of stamps on some parcels.

Number of stamps	1	2	3	4
Number of parcels	5	6	9	4

Find the mean number of stamps per parcel.

$\text{Mean} = \dfrac{\text{Total number of stamps}}{\text{Number of parcels}}$

$= \dfrac{1 \times 5 + 2 \times 6 + 3 \times 9 + 4 \times 4}{5 + 6 + 9 + 4}$

$= \dfrac{60}{24} = 2.5$

● Choosing the best average to use:
   When the most **popular** value is wanted use the **mode**.
   When **half** of the values have to be above the average use the **median**.
   When a **typical** value is wanted use either the **mode** or the **median**.
   When all the **actual** values have to be taken into account use the **mean**.
   When the average should not be distorted by a few very small or very large values do **not** use the mean.

Exercise 3   Do not use a calculator for questions 1 to 3.

1 Nine students were asked to estimate the length of this line, correct to the nearest centimetre.

The estimates the students made are shown.

$$8 \quad 10 \quad 10 \quad 10 \quad 11 \quad 12 \quad 12 \quad 14 \quad 15$$

(a) What is the range in their estimates?
(b) Which estimate is the mode?
(c) Which estimate is the median?
(d) Work out the mean of their estimates.

2 The prices paid for eight different meals at a restaurant are:

£10   £9   £9.50   £12   £20   £11.50   £11   £9

(a) Which price is the mode?   (b) Find the median price.   (c) Calculate the mean price.
(d) Which of these averages best describes the average price paid for a meal?
Give a reason for your answer.

3 (a) Calculate the mean of 13.9, 15.3, 11.7 and 16.2.
(b) Using your result from part (a),
explain how to find quickly the mean of 14.9, 16.3, 12.7 and 17.2
(c) Calculate the median of the numbers in part (a).
(d) If the number 16.2 in part (a) was changed to 27.2, explain, without doing a calculation,
whether the mean or the median would be more affected.   AQA

4 (a) The number of hours of sunshine each day last week is shown.

Monday	Tuesday	Wednesday	Thursday	Friday	Saturday	Sunday
5.3	6.4	3.7	4.8	7.5	8.6	5.7

(i) What is the range in the number of hours of sunshine each day?
(ii) Work out the mean number of hours of sunshine each day.
(b) In the same week last year, the range in the number of hours of sunshine each day was
9 hours and the mean was 3.5 hours.
Compare the number of hours of sunshine each day in these two weeks.

5 The graph shows the distribution of goals scored by a football team in home and away matches.

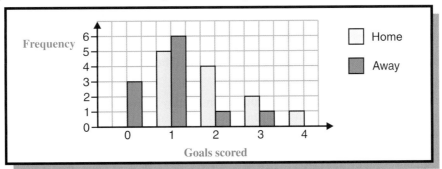

(a) What is the range of the number of goals scored at home matches?
(b) Calculate the mean number of goals per match for home matches.
(c) A supporter says, "The average number of goals per match is the same for both away
matches and home matches." Which average is being used?   AQA

6 Four taxi drivers recorded how many passengers they carried on each journey one evening.
The table shows the results.

		Number of passengers carried			
		1	2	3	4
Taxi	A	6	6	4	0
	B	7	7	3	1
	C	5	7	2	0
	D	4	4	3	1

(a) Which taxi completed the most journeys?
(b) Calculate the total number of journeys in which exactly 3 passengers were carried.
(c) There were 60 journeys made altogether.
Calculate the mean number of passengers per taxi journey.   AQA

Averages and Range

Presentation of Data 2

What you need to know

- A **time series** is a set of readings taken at time intervals.
- A **line graph** is used to show a time series.

Eg 1 The table shows the temperature of a patient taken every half-hour.

Time	0930	1000	1030	1100	1130	1200
Temperature °C	36.9	37.1	37.6	37.2	36.5	37.0

(a) Draw a line graph to illustrate the data.
(b) Estimate the patient's temperature at 1115.

(a)

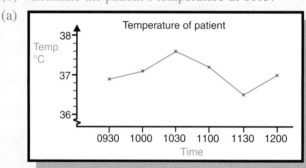

To draw a line graph:
Plot the given values.
Points are joined by lines to show the **trend**.

(b) 36.8°C

Only the plotted points represent **actual values**.
The lines show the **trend** and can be used to **estimate values**.

- **Histogram**. Used to illustrate **grouped frequency distributions.**
  The horizontal axis is a continuous scale.

- **Frequency polygon**. Used to illustrate grouped frequency distributions.
  Often used to compare two or more distributions on the same diagram.
  Frequencies are plotted at the midpoints of the class intervals and joined with straight lines.
  The horizontal axis is a continuous scale.

Eg 2 The frequency distribution of the heights of some boys is shown.

Height (h cm)	$130 \leqslant h < 140$	$140 \leqslant h < 150$	$150 \leqslant h < 160$	$160 \leqslant h < 170$	$170 \leqslant h < 180$
Frequency	1	7	12	9	3

Draw a histogram and a frequency polygon to illustrate the data.

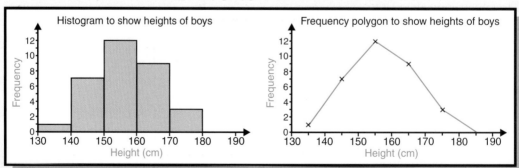

- **Misleading graphs**. Graphs may be misleading if:
  the scales are not labelled,   the scales are not uniform,   the frequency does not begin at zero.

1 On Sunday, Alfie records the outside temperature every two hours.
The temperatures he recorded are shown in the table.

Time of day	0800	1000	1200	1400	1600	1800
Outside temperature (°C)	9	12	15	17	16	14

(a) Draw a line graph to represent the data.
(b) What is the range in the temperatures recorded?
(c) (i) Use your graph to estimate the temperature at 1300.
   (ii) Explain why your answer in (c)(i) is an estimate.

2 The amount of time spent by a group of pupils on their mobile phones in one week is recorded.
Here are the results.

Time (minutes)	Number of pupils
Less than 10 minutes	12
10 minutes or more but less than 20 minutes	9
20 minutes or more but less than 30 minutes	13
30 minutes or more but less than 40 minutes	6
40 minutes or more but less than 50 minutes	8
50 minutes or more but less than 60 minutes	2

(a) State the modal class.
(b) Draw a histogram to show this information.   AQA

3 The number of words in the first 100 sentences of a book are shown in the table.

Number of words	1 to 10	11 to 20	21 to 30	31 to 40	41 to 50
Frequency	45	38	12	4	1

Draw a frequency polygon for these data.   AQA

4 The table shows the times of arrival of pupils at a village primary school one day.

Time of arrival (t)	$0830 \leqslant t < 0840$	$0840 \leqslant t < 0850$	$0850 \leqslant t < 0900$	$0900 \leqslant t < 0910$
Number of pupils	14	28	34	4

(a) Draw a frequency diagram for the data.
(b) Pupils arriving after 0900 are late.
   What percentage of pupils were late?

5 The graph shows the time taken to score the first goal in 20 football matches.

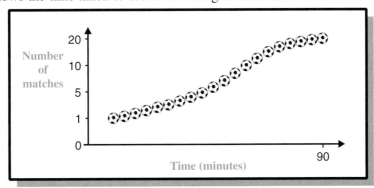

Explain why the graph is misleading.

Scatter Graphs ●●●●●●●●●●●●

What you need to know

- A **scatter graph** can be used to show the relationship between two sets of data.

- The relationship between two sets of data is referred to as **correlation**.

- You should be able to recognise **positive** and **negative** correlation. The correlation is stronger as points get closer to a straight line.

- When there is a relationship between two sets of data a **line of best fit** can be drawn on the scatter graph.

- The line of best fit can be used to **estimate** the value from one set of the data when the corresponding value of the other set is known.

Positive correlation   **Negative correlation**

Eg 1 | The table shows the weights and heights of 10 girls.

Weight (kg)	33	36	37	39	40	42	45	45	48	48
Height (cm)	133	134	137	140	146	146	145	150	152	156

(a) Draw a scatter graph for the data.
(c) What type of correlation is shown?

(b) Describe what the scatter graph shows.
(d) Draw a line of best fit.

Mark a cross on the graph to show the weight and height of each girl.

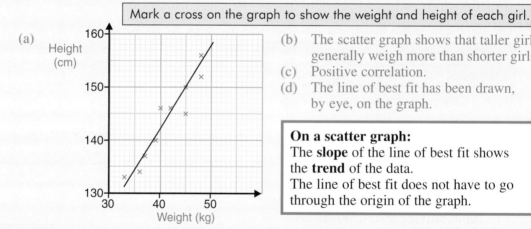

(a)

(b) The scatter graph shows that taller girls generally weigh more than shorter girls.
(c) Positive correlation.
(d) The line of best fit has been drawn, by eye, on the graph.

On a scatter graph:
The **slope** of the line of best fit shows the **trend** of the data.
The line of best fit does not have to go through the origin of the graph.

Exercise 5

1 The table gives information about the engine size (in cc's) and the fuel economy (in kilometres per litre) of a number of cars.

Engine size (cc)	1800	1000	1200	1600	1400	800	2000	1500
Fuel economy (km/l)	6.5	11	10.5	8	9.5	12	6	8.5

(a) Draw a scatter graph to show this information.
    Label the horizontal axis **Engine size (cc)** from 600 to 2000.
    Label the vertical axis **Fuel economy (km/l)** from 5 to 15.
(b) Describe the relationship between engine size and fuel economy.
(c) Draw a line of best fit.
(d) Explain how you can tell the relationship is quite strong.

2 The scatter graphs below show the results of a questionnaire given to pupils who have jobs.

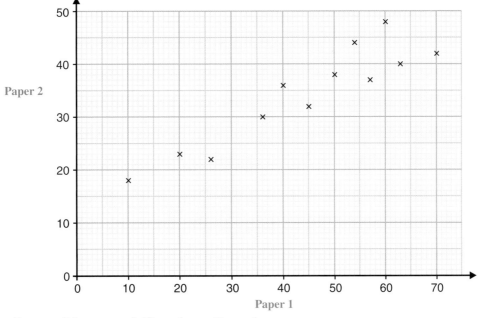

Diagram A — Number of hours worked

Diagram B — Number of hours worked

Diagram C — Number of hours worked

(a) Which scatter graph shows the number of hours worked plotted against:
   (i) the earnings of pupils,   (ii) the time spent by pupils watching TV,
   (iii) the time taken by pupils to travel to work?
(b) State which one of the graphs shows a negative correlation.

AQA

3 The scatter graph shows the results of candidates in two examinations in the same subject.

(a) One candidate scored 40 marks on Paper 1.
   What mark did this candidate score on Paper 2?
(b) One candidate scored 48 marks on Paper 2.
   What mark did this candidate score on Paper 1?
(c) Was the highest mark on both papers scored by the same candidate?
(d) Was the lowest mark on both papers scored by the same candidate?
(e) What type of correlation is there between the marks scored on the two exam papers?

4 The marks for 10 students in examinations in French and German are shown.

Mark in French	19	25	30	35	44	45	55	60	63	71
Mark in German	35	38	39	45	50	54	60	65	64	72

(a) Use this information to draw a scatter graph.
(b) What type of correlation is there between the marks in French and German?
(c) Draw a line of best fit.
(d) A student scored 50 marks in the French examination but was absent for the
   German examination.
   Estimate the mark this student might have scored if he had taken the German examination.

AQA

Probability

What you need to know

- **Probability** describes how likely or unlikely it is that an event will occur.
  Probabilities can be shown on a probability scale.

  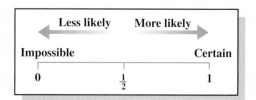

  Probability **must** be written as a **fraction**, a **decimal** or a **percentage**.

- How to work out probabilities using **equally likely outcomes**.

  $$\text{The probability of an event} = \frac{\text{Number of outcomes in the event}}{\text{Total number of possible outcomes}}$$

  Eg 1 A box contains 7 red pens and 4 blue pens. A pen is taken from the box at random.
  What is the probability that the pen is blue?

  $$P(\text{blue}) = \frac{\text{Number of blue pens}}{\text{Total number of pens}} = \frac{4}{11}$$

  P(blue) stands for the probability that the pen is blue.

- How to use probabilities to **estimate** the number of times an event occurs in an **experiment** or **observation**.

  $$\text{Estimate} = \text{total number of trials (or observations)} \times \text{probability of event}$$

  Eg 2 1000 raffle tickets are sold. Alan buys some tickets.
  The probability that Alan wins first prize is $\frac{1}{50}$.
  How many tickets did Alan buy?   Number of tickets $= 1000 \times \frac{1}{50} = 20$

- **Mutually exclusive events** cannot occur at the same time.

  When A and B are mutually exclusive events: $P(A \text{ or } B) = P(A) + P(B)$

  Eg 3 A box contains red, green, blue and yellow counters.
  The table shows the probability of getting each colour.

Colour	Red	Green	Blue	Yellow
Probability	0.4	0.25	0.25	0.1

  A counter is taken from the box at random.
  What is the probability of getting a red or blue counter?
  $P(\text{Red or Blue}) = P(\text{Red}) + P(\text{Blue}) = 0.4 + 0.25 = 0.65$

- The probability of an event, A, **not happening** is: $P(\text{not } A) = 1 - P(A)$

  Eg 4 Kathy takes a sweet from a bag at random.
  The probability that it is a toffee is 0.3.
  What is the probability that it is **not** a toffee?
  $P(\text{not toffee}) = 1 - P(\text{toffee}) = 1 - 0.3 = 0.7$

- How to find all the possible outcomes when two events are combined.
  By **listing** the outcomes systematically. By using a **possibility space diagram**.

1 An adult is chosen at random in Liverpool.
The probabilities of four events are marked on the probability scale.

     A: The adult is a female.   **C:** The adult is in Liverpool.

     B: The adult was born in France.   **D:** The adult is left-handed.

(a) Copy the scale and label each arrow with the correct letter.
(b) Use the scale to estimate the probability that the adult is left-handed.
(c) Estimate the probability that the adult is **not** left-handed.   AQA

2 A packet contains 1 red balloon, 3 white balloons and 4 blue balloons.
A balloon is taken from the packet at random.
(a) What is the probability that it is red?
(b) What is the probability that it is red or white?
(c) What is the probability that it is not white?

3 The diagram shows two sets of cards.
One card is taken from each set at random.

(a) List all the possible outcomes.
(b) The numbers on the cards are added together to give a score.
    What is the probability of getting a score of 6?   AQA

4 Petra has 5 numbered cards. She uses the cards to do this experiment:

> Shuffle the cards and then record the number on the top card.

She repeats the experiment 20 times and gets these results.

3   3   2   3   4   3   5   2   3   4   3   5   3   3   4   2   5   3   4   2

(a) What numbers do you think are on the five cards? Give a reason for your answer.
(b) She repeats the experiment 500 times.
    Estimate the number of times she will get a 5. Give a reason for your answer.

5 The table shows information about the colour and type of symbol printed on some cards.

		Colour of symbol		
		Red	**Yellow**	**Blue**
Type of	**O**	9	4	5
symbol	**X**	2	7	3

(a) A card is taken at random.
  (i) What is the probability that it has a red symbol?
  (ii) What is the probability that it has a blue symbol **or** an X?

(b) A yellow card is taken at random.
    What is the probability that it has the symbol X?   AQA

6 A box contains counters. The counters are numbered 1, 2, 3, 4 or 5.
A counter is taken from the box at random.
(a) Copy and complete the table to show the probability of each number being chosen.

Number on counter	1	2	3	4	5
Probability	0.20	0.30	0.15		0.10

(b) Is the number on the counter chosen more likely to be odd or even?
    You must show your working.   AQA

Probability . . . Probability . . . Probability . . .

1 The pictogram shows the number of videos hired from a shop each day last week.

Monday	◯◯ ◯
Tuesday	◯◯ ◯◯
Wednesday	◯◯ ◠
Thursday	◯◯ ◯◯ ◯◠
Friday	◯◯ ◯◯ ◯◯ ◯◯ ◯
Saturday	

On Monday 6 videos were hired.

(a) How many videos does ◯◯ represent?

(b) How many videos were hired on Thursday?

70 videos were hired altogether last week.

(c) How many videos were hired on Saturday?

2 Paige did a survey about pets. She asked each person, "How many pets do you have?" Here are her results.

3	2	1	1	4	2	3	1	0	0	1	3	0
1	4	2	0	1	5	1	2	4	1	4	2	

(a) Copy and complete the frequency table for this data.

Number of pets	Tally	Frequency
0		
1		

(b) Draw a bar chart to show this data.

3 The results of a survey of the holiday destinations of people booking holidays abroad are shown in the bar chart.

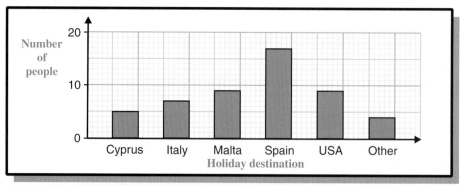

(a) Which holiday destination is the mode?

(b) How many more people are going to Spain than to Cyprus?

(c) How many people are included in the survey?

4 Vikram records the number of tennis matches won by each of ten players.

His results are: 8, 7, 9, 9, 4, 2, 8, 2, 3, 8.

(a) Write down the mode.
(b) Work out the median.
(c) Calculate the mean.
(d) Find the range.   AQA

5 The graph shows the distribution of the best height jumped by each girl in a high jump competition.

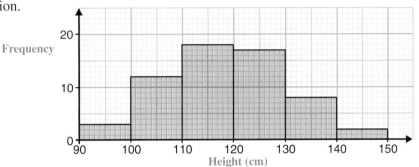

(a) How many girls jumped less than 100 cm?
(b) How many girls jumped between 100 cm and 120 cm?
(c) How many girls took part in the competition?

6 Sylvester did a survey to find the most popular pantomime.

(a) The results for children are shown in the table.

Pantomime	Aladdin	Cinderella	Jack and the Bean Stalk	Peter Pan
Number of children	45	35	25	15

(i) Draw a clearly labelled pie chart to illustrate this information.
(ii) Which pantomime is the mode?

(b) The results for adults are shown in the pie chart.
   (i) 20 adults chose Aladdin.
       How many adults were included in the survey?
   (ii) What percentage of adults chose Cinderella?

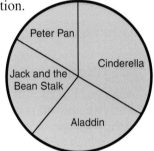

7 Karl plays a game with a spinner.
The spinner has three equal sections, coloured red, yellow and blue.
Karl spins the spinner twice.
If both spins land on the same colour, Karl wins 2 tokens.
If exactly one of the spins lands on red, Karl wins 1 token.
For any other result, Karl wins 0 tokens.

(a) Copy and complete the table to show the numbers of tokens that Karl can win.

		Second spin		
		Red	Yellow	Blue
First spin	Red			
	Yellow			
	Blue			

(b) What is the probability that Karl wins 0 tokens?
(c) Karl plays the game 70 times. How many times should he expect to win 2 tokens?   AQA

8 Linzi is doing a survey to find if there should be a supermarket in her neighbourhood.
This is one of her questions.

> "Do you agree that having a supermarket in the neighbourhood would make it easier for you to do your shopping and if we did have one would you use it?"

Give two reasons why this question is unsuitable in its present form.

9 A teacher asked the pupils in his maths class how long they had spent revising for a maths test.
He drew a scatter graph to compare their test results and the time they had spent revising.

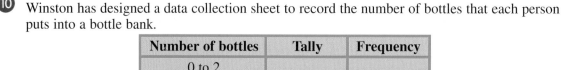

(a) State which point A, B, C or D represents the statement:
    (i)   Keith, "Even though I spent a long time revising, I still got a poor test result."
    (ii) Val, "I got a good test result despite not doing much revision."
    (iii) Jane, "I revised for ages and got a good test result."
(b) Make up a statement which matches the point you have **not** used in your answer to part (a).
(c) What does the scatter graph tell you about the relationship between the time the pupils spent revising and their test results?

AQA

10 Winston has designed a data collection sheet to record the number of bottles that each person puts into a bottle bank.

Number of bottles	Tally	Frequency
0 to 2		
3 to 6		
6 to 8		

(a) Give **three** criticisms of the class intervals that Winston has chosen.

Anna and Patrick watch people using the bottle bank.
Anna watches 60 people and calculates the mean to be 8.5 bottles per person.
Patrick watches 15 people and calculates the mean to be 9.2 bottles per person.
(b) Which of the two means would you expect to give the more reliable estimate of the mean number of bottles per person? Give a reason for your answer.

AQA

11 The lengths of 20 bolts, in centimetres, is shown.

    7.4   5.8   4.5   5.0   6.5   6.6   7.0   5.4   4.8   6.4
    5.4   6.2   7.2   5.5   4.8   6.5   5.0   6.0   6.5   6.8

(a) Draw a stem and leaf diagram to illustrate this information.
(b) What is the range in the lengths of these bolts?

12 The table shows information about a group of students.

	Can speak French	Cannot speak French
Male	5	20
Female	12	38

(a) One of these students is chosen at random.
What is the probability that the student can speak French?
(b) Pru says, "If a female student is chosen at random she is more likely to be able to speak French than if a male student is chosen at random." Is she correct? Explain your answer.

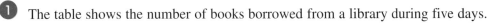
1 The table shows the number of books borrowed from a library during five days.

Day	Monday	Tuesday	Wednesday	Thursday	Friday
Number of books	40	35	30	15	50

(a) How many books were borrowed during these five days?

(b) Draw a pictogram to represent the information. Use [📖] to represent 10 books.

2 Five children guess the score on the next throw of a fair six-sided dice.

Abdul: It will be an even number.   Barbara: It will be a five.

David: It will be a seven.   Cathy: It will be less than five.

Ewan: It will be a number less than seven.

The scale shows the probability of each statement being correct.

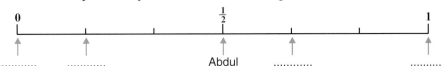

Copy the scale and fill in the names of the children. Abdul's has been done for you.   AQA

3 Nine people were asked to estimate the height, in metres, of a building.
The estimates the people made are shown.

      7   12   10   9   11   12   10   12   11

(a) Which height is the mode?

(b) Work out the median height.

(c) Calculate the mean height.   AQA

4 Pat carried out a survey.
She asked each pupil in her class how many postcards they received last August.
Her results are shown in the vertical line graph.

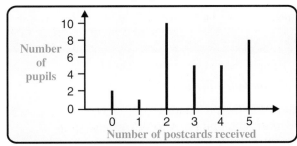

(a) What is the modal number of postcards received?

(b) How many pupils took part in the survey?

(c) How many postcards were received altogether?   AQA

5 Karina is playing a game with these cards. $\boxed{X}$ $\boxed{Y}$ $\boxed{1}$ $\boxed{1}$ $\boxed{3}$

One card is taken at random from the letters.
One card is taken at random from the numbers.

(a) List all the possible outcomes.

(b) Explain why the probability of getting   is not $\frac{1}{4}$.

6 The table shows the number of peas in a sample of pods.

Number of peas	1	2	3	4	5	6	7	8
Number of pods	0	0	2	3	5	7	2	1

(a) How many pods were in the sample?
(b) What is the modal number of peas in a pod?
(c) What is the range in the number of peas in a pod?
(d) Draw a bar chart to show this information.

7 The stem and leaf diagram shows the weights, in grams, of letters posted by a secretary.

1 | 5 means 15 grams

```
1 | 5  8
2 | 0  4  5  6  8  8
3 | 1  2  3  5  7
4 | 2  5
```

(a) How many letters were posted?
(b) What is the median weight of one of these letters?
(c) What is the range in the weights of these letters?
(d) Calculate the mean weight of a letter?

8 The bar chart shows the amount of time Year 6 pupils spend doing homework and watching television.

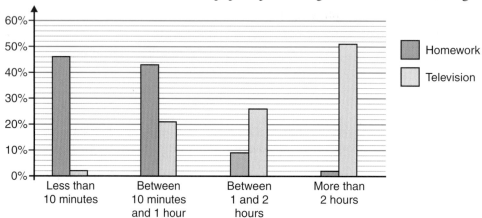

(a) What percentage of these pupils spend more than 2 hours watching television?
(b) Use the bar chart to complete this table for 'Time doing homework'.

Time doing homework	Less than 10 minutes	Between 10 minutes and 1 hour	Between 1 and 2 hours	More than 2 hours
Percentage of Year 6 pupils	46%			

(c) In a survey, Year 11 pupils were asked the question:

"Where do you learn the most?"

Their replies are shown in the pie chart.
(i) What was the most common reply to the question?
(ii) What percentage of pupils said they learnt most from television?
(iii) What fraction of the pupils said they learnt most at home?

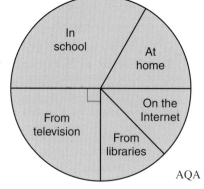

AQA

9 A bag contains 50 cubes of which 7 are red. A cube is taken from the bag at random.
(a) The probability that it is white is 0.3.
What is the probability that it is not white?
(b) What is the probability that it is either white or red?

16

10 The table shows the number of people in the UK with a full-time job.

Year	1980	1984	1988	1992	1996	2000
Number of people with a full-time job (millions)	18.7	19.1	20.5	19.3	18.5	19.3

(a) Use this information to draw a time series graph.
(b) Estimate the number of people in the UK with a full-time job in 1997. AQA

11 The table shows the results of asking 480 people how they travel to work.

Method of travel	Bus	Train	Car	Walk
Number of people	120	80	180	100

Draw a clearly labelled pie chart to represent this information. AQA

12 Mary has a bag in which there are 8 marbles, all green.
Tony has a bag in which there are 12 marbles, all red.
Jane has a bag in which there are some blue marbles.
(a) What is the probability of picking a red marble from Mary's bag?
(b) Mary and Tony put all their marbles into a box.
What is the probability of choosing a red marble from the box?
(c) Jane now adds her blue marbles to the box.
The probability of choosing a blue marble from the box is now $\frac{1}{2}$.
How many blue marbles does Jane put in the box? AQA

13 The numbers of people exposed to different types of
radiation in the UK were recorded.
The pie chart shows the results.

If 12 000 people were exposed to Gamma radiation
last year, estimate the total number of people who
were exposed to any form of radiation last year.

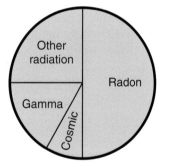

AQA

14 The mean weight of 7 netball players is 51.4 kg.
(a) Find the total weight of the players.

The mean weight of the 7 players and the reserve is 52.3 kg.
(b) Calculate the weight of the reserve. AQA

15 Corrin throws a dice 40 times. Her results are shown.

Score	1	2	3	4	5	6
Frequency	7	6	7	6	6	8

(a) Which score is the mode?
(b) Calculate the mean score.
(c) What is the median score?

16 A hospital carries out a test to compare the reaction times of patients of different ages.
The results are shown.

Age in years	17	21	24	25	31	15	18	29	20	26
Time (hundredths of a second)	29	40	45	65	66	21	33	62	32	53

(a) Plot the results as a scatter graph.
(b) What does the scatter graph tell you about the reaction times of these patients?
(c) Draw a line of best fit on the scatter graph.
(d) The hospital is worried about the reaction time of one patient.
How old is the patient? Give a reason for your answer. AQA

Whole Numbers 1

What you need to know

- You should be able to read and write numbers expressed in figures and words.

  Eg 1 The number 8543 is written or read as, "eight thousand five hundred and forty-three".

- Be able to order whole numbers.

  Eg 2 Write the numbers 17, 9, 35, 106 and 49 in ascending order.

  9, 17, 35, 49, 106

Smallest number	ascending order	Largest number
Largest number	descending order	Smallest number

- Be able to recognise the place value of each digit in a number.

  Eg 3 In the number 5384 the digit 8 is worth 80, but in the number 4853 the digit 8 is worth 800.

- Use mental methods to carry out addition and subtraction.

- Know the Multiplication Tables up to 10×10.

- Be able to: multiply whole numbers by 10, 100, 1000, …
  multiply whole numbers by 20, 30, 40, …
  divide whole numbers by 10, 100, 1000, …
  divide whole numbers by 20, 30, 40, …

×	1	2	3	4	5	6	7	8	9	10
1	1	2	3	4	5	6	7	8	9	10
2	2	4	6	8	10	12	14	16	18	20
3	3	6	9	12	15	18	21	24	27	30
4	4	8	12	16	20	24	28	32	36	40
5	5	10	15	20	25	30	35	40	45	50
6	6	12	18	24	30	36	42	48	54	60
7	7	14	21	28	35	42	49	56	63	70
8	8	16	24	32	40	48	56	64	72	80
9	9	18	27	36	45	54	63	72	81	90
10	10	20	30	40	50	60	70	80	90	100

Eg 4 Work out.   (a) 75×100
$= 7500$

(b) 42×30
$= 42 \times 10 \times 3$
$= 420 \times 3$
$= 1260$

Eg 5 Work out.   (a) $460 \div 10$
$= 46$

(b) $750 \div 30$
$= (750 \div 10) \div 3$
$= 75 \div 3$
$= 25$

- Use non-calculator methods for addition, subtraction, multiplication and division.

Eg 6 $476 + 254$

$$\begin{array}{r} 476 \\ + 254 \\ \hline 730 \\ \hline \tiny 1\ 1 \end{array}$$

Eg 7 $374 - 147$

$$\begin{array}{r} 3\overset{6}{\cancel{7}}{}^{1}4 \\ - 147 \\ \hline 227 \end{array}$$

Addition and Subtraction
Write the numbers in columns according to place value.
You can use addition to check your subtraction.

Eg 8 324×13

$$\begin{array}{r} 324 \\ \times 13 \\ \hline 972 \\ + 3240 \\ \hline 4212 \\ \hline \tiny 1\ 1 \end{array}$$

Long multiplication
Multiply by the units figure, then the tens figure, and so on.
Then add these answers.

Eg 9 $343 \div 7$

$$\begin{array}{r} 49 \\ 7\overline{)343} \\ 28 \\ \hline 63 \\ 63 \\ \hline 0 \end{array}$$

Long division
÷ (Obtain biggest answer possible.)
Calculate the remainder.
Bring down the next figure and repeat the process until there are no more figures to be brought down.

1 Write "six hundred and five thousand two hundred and thirty" in figures.

2 Write the numbers 85, 9, 23, 117 and 100 in descending order.

3 (a) In the number 23 547 the 4 represents 4 tens. What does the 3 represent?
(b) Write the number 23 547 in words.

4 (a) What must be added to 19 to make 100?
(b) What are the missing values?
    (i) $100 - 65 = \square$ (ii) $12 \times \square = 1200$ (iii) $150 \div \square = 15$

5 Work out. (a) $769 + 236$ (b) $400 - 209$ (c) $258 - 75$

6 (a) By using each of the digits 8, 5, 2 and 3 write down
    (i)   the smallest four-digit number,
    (ii) the largest four-digit number.
(b) What is the answer when you subtract the smallest number from the largest number?

7 The chart shows the distances in kilometres between some towns.

Tony drives from Poole to Bath and then from Bath to Selby.
(a) How far does Tony drive?

Jean drives from Poole to Woking
and then from Woking to Selby.
(b) Whose journey is longer?
    How much further is it?

Bath			
104	Poole		
153	133	Woking	
362	452	367	Selby

8 Work out. (a) 200×60 (b) $40\,000 \div 80$ (c) 25×7 (d) $45 \div 3$

9 The table shows the money Jayne has saved in her money box.

Value of coin	5p	10p	20p	50p
Number of coins	6	12	5	3

How much money has Jayne saved altogether?   AQA

10

The Lucky Club has 150 members.
Each member pays £15 per year.

(a) How much does the club receive altogether in 1 year?

(b) What is the total paid out in prizes in 1 year?

(c) How much profit does the club make in 1 year?   AQA

11 Last year Mr Alderton had the following household bills.

Gas	£364	Electricity	£158	Telephone	£187
Water	£244	Insurance	£236	Council Tax	£983

He paid the bills by 12 equal monthly payments.
How much was each monthly payment?

12 James packs teddy bears into boxes.
He packs 283 teddy bears every hour.
James works 47 hours in one week.
How many teddy bears does James pack in this week?   AQA

Whole Numbers 2

 **What you need to know**

- Know the order of operations in a calculation.

First	Brackets and Division line
Second	Divide and Multiply
Third	Addition and Subtraction

Eg 1 $4 + 2 \times 6 = 4 + 12 = 16$

Eg 2 $9 \times (7 - 2) + 3 = 9 \times 5 + 3 = 45 + 3 = 48$

- A number can be rounded to an **approximate** number.

- How to **round** to the nearest 10, 100, 1000.

  Eg 3 Write 6473 to (a) the nearest 10, (b) the nearest 100, (c) the nearest 1000.

  (a) 6470   (b) 6500   (c) 6000

- In real-life problems a rounding must be used which gives a commonsense answer.

  Eg 4 Doughnuts are sold in packets of 6. Tessa needs 20 doughnuts for a party. How many packets of doughnuts must she buy?

  $20 \div 6 = 3.33\ldots$ This should be rounded up to 4. So, Tessa must buy 4 packets.

- How to approximate to one **significant figure**.

  - Identify the most significant figure.
  - Look at the next figure to the right of this and
     if the figure is 5 or more round up,
     if the figure is less than 5 round down.
  - Add noughts, as necessary, to preserve place value.

  Eg 5 Write each of these numbers correct to 1 significant figure.

  (a) 365   (b) 82

  (a) 400   (b) 80

- You should be able to use approximations to estimate that the actual answer to a calculation is of the right order of magnitude.

  Estimation is done by approximating every number in the calculation to one significant figure. The calculation is then done using the approximated values.

  Eg 6 Use approximations to estimate $\dfrac{51 \times 572}{98}$.

  $\dfrac{51 \times 572}{98} = \dfrac{50 \times 600}{100} = 300$

- Be able to use a calculator to check answers to calculations.

- An expression such as $5 \times 5 \times 5$ can be written in a shorthand way as 5^3. This is read as '5 to the power of 3'.

- Numbers raised to the power of 2 are **squared**.

  Square numbers are whole numbers squared.
  The first few square numbers are: 1, 4, 9, 16, 25, 36, ...

  Squares can be calculated using the $\boxed{x^2}$ button on a calculator.

  Eg 7 $4^2 = 4 \times 4 = 16$

- Numbers raised to the power of 3 are **cubed**.

  Cube numbers are whole numbers cubed.
  The first few cube numbers are: 1, 8, 27, 64, 125, ...

  Eg 8 $4^3 = 4 \times 4 \times 4 = 64$

- **Powers**
  The squares and cubes of numbers can be worked out on a calculator by using the $\boxed{x^y}$ button.
  The $\boxed{x^y}$ button can be used to calculate the value of a number x raised to the power of y.

  Eg 9 Calculate 26^3.
  Enter the sequence: $\boxed{2}$ $\boxed{6}$ $\boxed{x^y}$ $\boxed{3}$ $\boxed{=}$. So $26^3 = 17576$

Exercise 8   Do not use a calculator for this exercise.

1 Work out. (a) $6 + 4 \times 3$ (b) $96 \div (3 + 5)$ (c) $2 \times (18 - 12) - 4$

2 Write these products in a shorthand way using powers.
(a) 9×9 (b) $10 \times 10 \times 10 \times 10 \times 10 \times 10$ (c) $7 \times 7 \times 7$

3 Work out: (a) the square of 5,   (b) the cube of 10.

4 Work out the value of (a) 4^2 (b) 5^3 (c) 10^4

5 Look at these numbers: 2   15   27   36   44   51   64   100   1000
(a) Which of these numbers are square numbers?
(b) Which of these numbers is both a square number and a cube number?

6 James thinks that when you square a number you always get an odd number answer.
Give an example to show that James is wrong.   AQA

7 Jenny says that $2^2 + 3^2 = (2 + 3)^2$.
Is she right? Show your working.

8 Find the value of (a) $1^2 + 2^2 + 3^2 + 4^2 + 5^2$ (b) $9^2 \times 10^2$ (c) $2^3 \times 5^2$

9 Richard says that $1^3 + 2^3 = 3^3$.
Is he right? Show your working.

10 Chris is 10 cm taller than Steven. Their heights add up to 310 cm. How tall is Steven?   AQA

11 Write the result shown on the calculator display
(a) to the nearest whole number,
(b) to the nearest ten,
(c) to the nearest hundred.

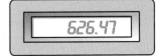
626.47

12 A newspaper's headline states: "20 000 people attend concert".
The number in the newspaper is given to the nearest thousand.
What is the smallest possible attendance?

13 The number of people at a football match was 36 743.
(a) How many people is this to the nearest hundred?
(b) How many people is this to the nearest thousand?

14 The diagram shows the distances between towns A, B and C.

A ← 287 km → B ← 114 km → C

By rounding each of the distances given to the nearest hundred, estimate the distance
between A and C.

15 A snack bar sells coffee at 48 pence per cup. In one day 838 cups are sold.
By rounding each number to one significant figure, estimate the total amount received from
the sale of coffee, giving your answer in pounds.   AQA

16 (a) 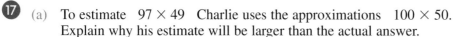 43 × 18 is about 800   Use approximation to show that this is correct.

(b) (i) Show how you could find an estimate for   2019 ÷ 37.
(ii) What is your estimated answer?

17 (a) To estimate   97 × 49   Charlie uses the approximations   100 × 50.
Explain why his estimate will be larger than the actual answer.
(b) To estimate   1067 ÷ 48   Patsy uses the approximations   1000 ÷ 50.
Will her estimate be larger or smaller than the actual answer?
Give a reason for your answer.

18 Isobella pays for 68 photographs to be developed. Each photograph costs 34 pence.
Isobella calculates the total cost to be £231.20.
(a) Which two numbers would you multiply to find a quick estimate of the total cost?
(b) Use your numbers to show whether Isobella's calculation could be correct.
Comment on your answer.

AQA

19 Melanie needs 200 crackers for an office party.
The crackers are sold in boxes of 12.
How many boxes must she buy?

20 Mrs. Preece is printing an examination for all Year 11 students.
Each examination uses 14 sheets of paper.
(a) There are 235 students in Year 11.
How many sheets of paper does she need?
(b) A ream contains 500 sheets of paper.
How many reams of paper does she need to print all the examinations?

AQA

21 Wayne is calculating $\dfrac{8961}{1315 + 1692}$

(a) Write down each of the numbers   8961,   1315   and   1692   to the nearest hundred.

(b) Hence, estimate the value of $\dfrac{8961}{1315 + 1692}$

22 By rounding each of the numbers in this calculation to one significant figure,

estimate the value of $\dfrac{79 \times 492}{43}$.   Show your working.

23 Clint has to calculate $\dfrac{414 + 198}{36}$.

He calculates the answer to be   419.5.
By rounding each number to one significant figure estimate whether his answer is about right.
Show all your working.

24 (a) Find an approximate value of $\dfrac{21 \times 58}{112}$.

(b) Use a calculator to find the difference between your approximate value and the exact value.

25 In 2001 Mr Symms drove 8873 kilometres.
His car does 11 kilometres per litre. Petrol costs 69.9 pence per litre.
(a) By rounding each number to one significant figure, estimate the amount he spent on petrol.
(b) Without any further calculation, explain why this estimate will be larger than the actual
amount.

What you need to know

- You should be able to write decimals in order by considering place value.

  Eg 1 Write the decimals 4.1, 4.001, 4.15, 4.01, and 4.2
  in order, from the smallest to the largest.
  4.001, 4.01, 4.1, 4.15, 4.2

- Be able to use non-calculator methods to add and subtract decimals.

  Eg 2 $2.8 + 0.56$

$$\begin{array}{r} 2.8 \\ + 0.56 \\ \hline 3.36 \\ \hline \end{array}$$

  Eg 3 $9.5 - 0.74$

$$\begin{array}{r} \overset{8,\,14,\,1}{\cancel{9.5}0} \\ - 0.74 \\ \hline 8.76 \\ \hline \end{array}$$

  Addition and Subtraction
  Keep the decimal points in a vertical column.
  9.5 can be written as 9.50.

- You should be able to multiply and divide decimals by powers of 10 (10, 100, 1000, …)

  Eg 4 Work out. (a) 6.7×100 (b) 0.35×10 (c) $5.4 \div 10$ (d) $4.6 \div 100$
  $= 670$ $= 3.5$ $= 0.54$ $= 0.046$

- Be able to use non-calculator methods to multiply and divide decimals by other decimals.

  Eg 5 0.43×5.1

$$\begin{array}{r} 0.43 \quad (2\,\text{d.p.}) \\ \times \quad 5.1 \quad (1\,\text{d.p.}) \\ \hline 43 \leftarrow 43 \times 1 \\ + 2150 \leftarrow 43 \times 50 \\ \hline 2.193 \quad (3\,\text{d.p.}) \\ \hline \end{array}$$

  Multiplication
  Ignore the decimal points and multiply the numbers.
  Count the total number of decimal places in the question.
  The answer has the same total number of decimal places.

  Eg 6 $1.64 \div 0.2$
  $\frac{1.64}{0.2} = \frac{16.4}{2} = 8.2$

  Division
  It is easier to divide by a whole number than by a decimal.
  So, multiply the numerator and denominator by a power of 10 (10, 100, …) to make the dividing number a whole number.

- You should be able to change decimals to fractions.

  Eg 7 (a) $0.2 = \frac{2}{10} = \frac{1}{5}$ (b) $0.65 = \frac{65}{100} = \frac{13}{20}$ (c) $0.07 = \frac{7}{100}$

- How to approximate using **decimal places**.

  Write the number using one more decimal place than asked for.
  Look at the last decimal place and
  - if the figure is 5 or more round up,   - if the figure is less than 5 round down.

  Eg 8 Write the number 3.649 to (a) 2 decimal places,   (b) 1 decimal place.
  (a) 3.65   (b) 3.6

- You should be able to use decimal notation for money and other measures.

  The metric and common imperial units you need to know are given in Section 34.

- Be able to carry out a variety of calculations involving decimals.

Do not use a calculator for questions 1 to 10.

1 Look at this collection of numbers.
  (a) Which number is the largest?
  (b) Which number is the smallest?
  (c) Write the numbers in ascending order.
  (d) Two of these numbers are multiplied together.
      Which two numbers will give the smallest answer?

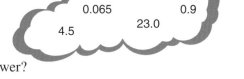

13.5   0.065   0.9   4.5   23.0

2 Work out. (a) $12.08 + 6.51$ (b) $6.8 + 4.57$ (c) $4.7 - 1.8$ (d) $5.0 - 2.3$

3 Ann flies from Manchester to Hong Kong.
  At Manchester Airport her case is weighed and the scales show 15.7 kg.
  In Hong Kong she buys four presents for her family.
  They weigh 4 kg, 2.50 kg, 0.75 kg, 3.60 kg.
  (a) What is the total weight of these presents in kilograms?
  (b) Ann puts the presents in her case when she packs it to fly home.
      What does it weigh now?
  (c) If her case now weighs more than 20kg, there is an extra charge.
      She has to pay 15 dollars for every kg or part kg over 20 kg.
      How much does Ann have to pay?

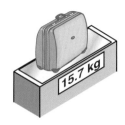

15.7 kg

AQA

4 Cakes cost 27 pence each.
  Lubna buys 5 cakes.
  She pays with a £10 note.
  How much change should she be given?

27p each

5 (a) Multiply 3.2 by 100.   (b) Divide 3.2 by 10.

6 (a) Work out the answer to this sum in your head. 900×0.6
      Explain clearly the method you used.
  (b) $40 \div 0.8$ Work out the answer to this sum in your head.
      Explain clearly the method you used.

AQA

7 Two pieces of wood of length 0.75 m and 2.68 m are sawn from a plank 5 m long.
  What length of wood is left?

8 Work out. (a) (i) 4×0.3 (ii) 4.8×2.5 (b) (i) $7 \div 0.5$ (ii) $2.94 \div 7$

9 Using the calculation $24 \times 26 = 624$, find the values which complete the three boxes.

$24 \times 26 = 624$

$48 \times 26 = \ldots\ldots$ $2.4 \times 2.6 = \ldots\ldots$ $62.4 \div 26 = \ldots\ldots$

AQA

10 Write as a fraction. (a) 0.3   (b) 0.03   (c) 0.33

11 Calculate $97.2 \div 6.5$.
  Give your answer correct to (a) two decimal places,   (b) one decimal place.

12 (a) Calculate 78.4×8.76.   (b) Give your answer to (a) correct to one significant figure.

13 David buys 0.6 kg of grapes and 0.5 kg of apples. He pays £1.36 altogether.
  The grapes cost £1.45 per kilogram. How much per kilogram are apples?

AQA

14 (a) Calculate $\dfrac{58.4 \times 19.6}{29.2 + 9.8}$ correct to two decimal places.
  (b) By rounding each number to one significant figure check that your answer to (a) is about
      right. You must show all your working.

Negative Numbers ●●●●●●●●●

What you need to know

- You should be able to use **negative numbers** in context, such as temperature, bank accounts.

- Realise where negative numbers come on a **number line**.

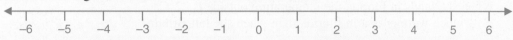

| As you move from left to right along the number line the numbers become bigger. | As you move from right to left along the number line the numbers become smaller. |

- Be able to put numbers in order (including negative numbers).

  Eg 1 Write the numbers $19, -3, 7, -5$ and 0 in ascending order.
  $$-5, \quad -3, \quad 0, \quad 7, \quad 19$$

- Add $(+)$, subtract $(-)$, multiply $(\times)$ and divide $(\div)$ with negative numbers.

  Eg 2 Work out.

  (a) $-3 + 10$ (b) $-5 - 7$ (c) -4×5 (d) $-12 \div 4$

  $= 7$ $= -12$ $= -20$ $= -3$

Exercise 10   Do not use a calculator for this exercise.

1 What temperatures are shown by these thermometers?

(a)    (b)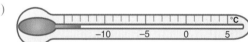

2 The midday temperatures in three different places on the same day are shown.

| Moscow $-7°C$ Oslo $-9°C$ Warsaw $-5°C$ |

(a) Which place was coldest?   (b) Which place was warmest?

3 The top of a cliff is 125 m above sea level.
The bottom of the lake is 15 m below sea level.
How far is the bottom of the lake below the
top of the cliff?

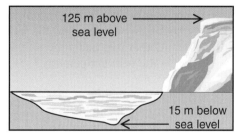

125 m above sea level

15 m below sea level

4 Place the following numbers in order of size, starting with the smallest.

$17 \quad -9 \quad -3 \quad 5 \quad 0 \quad 7$

5 Work out.   (a) $-5 + 10$ (b) $-10 - 5$ (c) -5×10 (d) $-10 \div 5$

6 What number must be placed in the box to complete each of the following?

(a) $-4 + \square = 2$ (b) $-2 - \square = -7$ (c) $\square \times 4 = -12$

7

| | | | | | | | | | °C |
| -20 | -10 | 0 | 10 | 20 | 30 | | | | |

Copy the scale.
Katy goes on holiday to Florida.

(a) When Katy gets on the plane in Britain the temperature outside is −5°C.
Mark this temperature on your scale with an arrow and label it *A*.

(b) Inside the plane is 18°C.
Mark this temperature on your scale with an arrow and label it *B*.

(c) How much warmer is it in the plane than outside?

(d) When she lands in Florida the temperature outside is 22°C.
How much warmer is it in Florida than when she left Britain?
AQA

8 Copy and complete this magic square, so that every row, column and diagonal adds up to 3.

2	−3	4
3	1	
−2		0

AQA

9 In Gdansk, Poland, the temperature on one day in January rose from −7°F to +22°F.
By how many degrees did the temperature rise?
AQA

10 Poppy's bank account is overdrawn by £79.
She pays in a cheque and then has a balance of £112.
How much has she paid into her bank account?
AQA

11 The table shows the temperatures recorded at a ski resort one day in February.

Time	0600	1200	1800	2400
Temperature (°C)	−3	3	−2	−6

(a) By how many degrees did the temperature rise between 0600 and 1200?

(b) During which six-hourly period was the maximum drop in temperature recorded?

12 Simon took some chicken pieces out of the freezer.
The temperature of the chicken pieces was −20°C.
Two hours later he measured the temperature of the chicken pieces to be −7°C.

(a) By how many degrees had the temperature risen?

(b) After another two hours the temperature had risen by the same amount again.
What is the new temperature?
AQA

13 The ice cream is stored at −25°C.
How many degrees is this below
the required storage temperature?

ICE CREAM
Store below
−18°C

14 This rule can be used to estimate the temperature in °F for temperatures given in °C.

Multiply the temperature in °C by 2 and add 30.

Use this rule to estimate −5°C in °F.

Fractions ●●●●●●●●●●●●●●●●●●●●●

What you need to know

- The top number of a fraction is called the **numerator**, the bottom number is called the **denominator**.

- Fractions which are equal are called **equivalent fractions**.

  To write an equivalent fraction:
  Multiply the numerator and denominator by the **same** number.

  Eg 1 $\dfrac{1}{4} = \dfrac{1 \times 3}{4 \times 3} = \dfrac{1 \times 5}{4 \times 5}$

  $\dfrac{1}{4} = \dfrac{3}{12} = \dfrac{5}{20}$

- Fractions can be **simplified** if both the numerator and denominator can be divided by the **same number**. This is sometimes called **cancelling**.

  Eg 2 Write the fraction $\dfrac{20}{28}$ in its simplest form.

  $\dfrac{20}{28} = \dfrac{20 \div 4}{28 \div 4} = \dfrac{5}{7}$

  Divide both the numerator and denominator by the largest number that divides into them both.

- $2\dfrac{1}{2}$ is an example of a **mixed number**. It is a mixture of whole numbers and fractions.

- $\dfrac{5}{2}$ is an **improper** (or '**top heavy**') fraction.

- Fractions must have the **same denominator** before **adding** or **subtracting**.

  Eg 3 Work out.

  (a) $\dfrac{3}{4} + \dfrac{2}{3} = \dfrac{9}{12} + \dfrac{8}{12} = \dfrac{17}{12} = 1\dfrac{5}{12}$

  (b) $\dfrac{4}{5} - \dfrac{1}{2} = \dfrac{8}{10} - \dfrac{5}{10} = \dfrac{3}{10}$

  Add (or subtract) the numerators only. When the answer is an improper fraction change it into a mixed number.

- You should be able to multiply and divide fractions.

  Eg 4 Work out.

  (a) $\dfrac{3}{4} \times 12 = \dfrac{3}{4} \times \dfrac{\cancel{12}^{3}}{1} = \dfrac{9}{1} = 9$

  The working can be simplified by dividing a numerator and a denominator by the same number.

  (b) $\dfrac{3}{4} \times \dfrac{1}{3} = \dfrac{\cancel{3}^{1}}{4} \times \dfrac{1}{\cancel{3}_{1}} = \dfrac{1}{4}$

  (c) $\dfrac{4}{5} \div 6 = \dfrac{\cancel{4}^{2}}{5} \times \dfrac{1}{\cancel{6}_{3}} = \dfrac{2}{15}$

  Dividing by 6 is the same as multiplying by $\dfrac{1}{6}$.

- All fractions can be written as decimals.

  To change a fraction to a decimal divide the **numerator** by the **denominator**.

  Eg 5 Change $\dfrac{4}{5}$ to a decimal.

  $\dfrac{4}{5} = 4 \div 5 = 0.8$

Exercise 11 — Do not use a calculator for this exercise.

1. (a) What fraction of this rectangle is shaded?

   (b) Copy and shade $\dfrac{2}{3}$ of this rectangle.

2 Which of the fractions $\frac{2}{5}$, $\frac{3}{8}$, $\frac{4}{12}$, $\frac{5}{15}$ are equivalent?

3 Which of these fractions are **not** equal to $\frac{1}{4}$?

$\frac{2}{8}$	$\frac{3}{9}$	$\frac{4}{16}$	$\frac{6}{24}$	$\frac{7}{35}$

4 (a) Which of the fractions $\frac{7}{10}$ or $\frac{4}{5}$ is the smaller? Explain why.

(b) Write down a fraction that lies halfway between $\frac{1}{3}$ and $\frac{1}{2}$.

5 Write these fractions in order of size, with the smallest first. $\quad\frac{2}{3}\quad\frac{5}{8}\quad\frac{7}{12}\quad\frac{3}{4}$ AQA

6 Stilton cheese costs £6.40 per kilogram. How much is $\frac{1}{4}$ kg of Stilton cheese?

7 This rule can be used to change kilometres into miles.

> Multiply the number of kilometres by $\frac{5}{8}$

Flik cycles 24 kilometres. How many miles is this?

8 Alec's cat eats $\frac{2}{3}$ of a tin of food each day.

What is the least number of tins Alec needs to buy to feed his cat for 7 days?   AQA

9 An examination is marked out of 48.
Ashley scored 32 marks.
What fraction of the total did he score?
Give your answer in its simplest form.

10 A garden centre buys 1000 Christmas trees. It sells $\frac{3}{5}$ of them at £8 each.

The remaining trees are then reduced to £5 each and all except 30 are sold.
These 30 trees are thrown away.
How much money does the garden centre get from selling the trees?   AQA

11 Work out.

(a) $\frac{3}{10} + 1\frac{4}{5}$ (b) $\frac{5}{8} - \frac{1}{2}$ (c) $\frac{2}{3} \times 24$ (d) $\frac{3}{4} \div 2$ (e) $\frac{4}{5} \times \frac{1}{2}$

12 Write these fractions as decimals.   (a) $\frac{1}{4}$ (b) $\frac{7}{10}$ (c) $\frac{3}{5}$ (d) $\frac{1}{8}$

13 (a) Change $\frac{1}{6}$ to a decimal. Give the answer correct to 3 d.p.

(b) Write these numbers in order of size, starting with the largest.

1.067	1.7	1.66	$1\frac{1}{6}$	1.67

14 (a) Work out $\frac{2}{3} \times \frac{1}{4}$ (b) Work out $\frac{2}{3} - \frac{1}{4}$ AQA

15 Debra spends $\frac{1}{3}$ of her pay on housekeeping, $\frac{2}{5}$ on travel and entertainment and saves the rest.
What fraction of her pay does she save?

16 $\frac{2}{5}$ of the people at a party are girls, $\frac{1}{4}$ of the girls are wearing fancy dress.
What fraction of the people at the party are girls wearing fancy dress?

Percentages ● ● ● ● ● ● ● ● ● ● ● ● ● ● ● ●

What you need to know

- 10% is read as '10 percent'. 'Per cent' means out of 100. 10% means 10 out of 100.

- A percentage can be written as a fraction, 10% can be written as $\frac{10}{100}$.

- To change a decimal or a fraction to a percentage: **multiply by 100**.

  Eg 1 Write as a percentage (a) 0.12   (b) $\frac{8}{25}$

  (a) $0.12 \times 100 = 12\%$ (b) $\frac{8}{25} \times 100 = 32\%$

- To change a percentage to a fraction or a decimal: **divide by 100**.

  Eg 2 Write 18% as (a) a decimal,   (b) a fraction.

  (a) $18\% = 18 \div 100 = 0.18$ (b) $18\% = \frac{18}{100} = \frac{9}{50}$

- How to express one quantity as a percentage of another.

  Eg 3 Write 30p as a percentage of £2.

  $\frac{30}{200} \times 100 = 30 \times 100 \div 200 = 15\%$

  Write the numbers as a fraction, using the same units. Change the fraction to a percentage.

- You should be able to use percentages to solve a variety of problems.

- Be able to find a percentage of a quantity.

  Eg 4 Find 20% of £64.
  £64 ÷ 100 = £0.64
  £0.64 × 20 = £12.80

  1. Divide by 100 to find 1%.
  2. Multiply by the percentage to be found.

- Be able to find a percentage increase (or decrease).

  Eg 5 Find the percentage loss on a micro-scooter bought for £25 and sold for £18.

  Percentage loss $= \frac{7}{25} \times 100 = 28\%$

  Percentage decrease $= \dfrac{\text{actual decrease}}{\text{initial value}} \times 100\%$

  Percentage increase $= \dfrac{\text{actual increase}}{\text{initial value}} \times 100\%$

Exercise 12

Do not use a calculator for questions 1 to 12.

1 What percentage of these rectangles are shaded?

(a)   (b)   (c)

2 Write $\frac{1}{2}$, 0.02 and 20% in order of size, smallest first.

3 Work out (a) 10% of 20 pence,   (b) 25% of 60 kg   (c) 5% of £900.

4 In an examination Felicity scored 75% of the marks and Daisy scored $\frac{4}{5}$ of the marks. Who has the better score? Give a reason for your answer.

5 Copy and complete this table.

Fraction	Decimal	Percentage
$\frac{3}{4}$	0.75	
	0.3	
$\frac{3}{5}$		

6 An athletics stadium has 35 000 seats.
4% of the seats are fitted with headphones to help people hear the announcements.
How many headphones are there in the stadium?

AQA

7 Jayne is given £50 for her birthday. She spends 30% of it.
How much of her birthday money does she spend?

AQA

8 A large candle costs £4. A medium candle costs 60% of this price.
How much does a medium candle cost?

AQA

9 180 college students apply for jobs at a new supermarket.
(a) 70% of the students are given an interview.
How many students are given an interview?
(b) 54 students are offered jobs.
What percentage of the students who applied were offered jobs?

10 What is (a) 60 pence as a percentage of £3, (b) 15 seconds as a percentage of 1 minute?

11

The original price of a tennis racket was £35.
What is the sale price of the tennis racket?

AQA

12 Mira earns £600 a week. She is given a 5% pay rise.
How much does she now earn a week?

13 Find 48% of £9.50.

14 A dress normally costs £35. The price is reduced by 15% in a sale.
What is the price of the dress in the sale?

AQA

15 Harvey sees this advertisement.
Calculate the actual price of the language course.

16 A snack bar buys sandwiches for £1.60 and sells them for 20% more.
What is the selling price of a packet of sandwiches at the snack bar?

17 In an experiment a spring is extended from 12 cm to 15 cm.
Calculate the percentage increase in the length of the spring.

18 You have to climb 123 steps to see the view from the top of a tower.

Harold has climbed 66 steps.
What percentage of the steps has he still got to climb?
Give your answer to the nearest whole number.

Time and Money

What you need to know

- Time can be given using either the **12-hour clock** or the **24-hour clock**.

  Eg 1 (a) 1120 is equivalent to 11.20 am.
  (b) 1645 is equivalent to 4.45 pm.

  > When using the 12-hour clock:
  > times **before** midday are given as am,
  > times **after** midday are given as pm.

- **Timetables** are usually given using the 24-hour clock.

  Eg 2 Some of the rail services from Manchester to Stoke are shown.

Manchester	0925	1115	1215	1415	1555
Stockport	0933	—	1223	—	1603
Stoke	1007	1155	1255	1459	1636

  > Some trains do not stop at every station. This is shown by a dash on the timetable.

  Kath catches the 1555 from Manchester to Stoke.
  (a) How many minutes does the journey take?
  (b) What is her arrival time in 12-hour clock time?

  (a) 41 minutes
  (b) 4.36 pm

- When considering a **best buy**, compare quantities by using the same units.

  Eg 3 Peanut butter is available in small or large jars.
  Small jar: 250 grams for 68 pence   Large jar: 454 grams for £1.25
  Which size is the better value for money?

  > Compare the number of grams per penny for each size.

  Small jar: $250 \div 68 \ = 3.67\ldots$ grams per penny
  Large jar: $454 \div 125 = 3.63\ldots$ grams per penny
  The small jar gives more grams per penny and is better value.

- **Value added tax**, or **VAT**, is a tax on some goods and services and is added to the bill.

  Eg 4 A freezer costs $£180 + 17\frac{1}{2}\%$ VAT.

  > $17\frac{1}{2}\% = 17.5\% = \dfrac{17.5}{100} = 0.175$

  (a) How much is the VAT?
  (b) What is the total cost of the freezer?

  (a) VAT $= £180 \times 0.175 = £31.50$
  (b) Total cost $= £180 + £31.50 = £211.50$

- **Exchange rates** are used to show what £1 will buy in foreign currencies.

  Eg 5 Alex buys a painting for 80 euros in France.
  The exchange rate is 1.55 euros to the £.
  What is the cost of the painting in £s?

  1.55 euros $= £1$ 80 euros $= 80 \div 1.55 = £51.6129\ldots$
  The painting cost £51.61, to the nearest penny.

Exercise 13

Do not use a calculator for questions 1 to 5.

1 Greta left home at 2.38 pm and walked for 15 minutes to a bus stop.
  (a) At what time did Greta arrive at the bus stop? Give your answer in 24-hour clock time.

  Her bus arrived at 3.12 pm.
  (b) How long did Greta have to wait for her bus?   AQA

2 Andy buys a box of chocolates which costs £3.57. He pays with a £20 note.
  (a) How much change does he receive?

  This change is given in the smallest number of notes and coins.
  (b) How is the change given?   AQA

3 The times of rail journeys from Guildford to Waterloo are shown.

Guildford	0703	0722	0730	0733	0749	0752
Worplesdon	0708	0727	—	0739	—	0757
Clapham Junction	0752	—	0800	0822	—	—
Waterloo	0800	0815	0808	0830	0823	0844

(a) Karen catches the 0722 from Guildford to Waterloo.
   How many minutes does the journey take?

(b) Graham arrives at Worplesdon station at 0715.
   What is the time of the next train to Clapham Junction?

4 A train travels from Grantham to London.
(a) The train leaves Grantham at 11.50. It arrives in London at 13.10.
   (i) Write these two times in 12-hour clock time.
   (ii) How long does the train journey take? Give your answer in hours and minutes.
(b) A family of 2 adults and 1 child travel from Grantham to London.
   The adult train fare is £17.68. A child's fare is half the adult's fare.
   What is the total cost of their fares?

AQA

5 Reg travels to Ireland. The exchange rate is 1.60 euros to the £.
(a) He changes £40 into euros.
   How many euros does he receive?
(b) A taxi fare costs 10 euros.
   What is the cost of the taxi fare in pounds and pence?

6

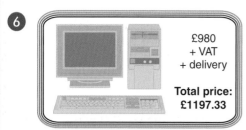

£980
+ VAT
+ delivery

Total price:
£1197.33

A computer is advertised at £980 + VAT + delivery.
VAT is charged at $17\frac{1}{2}$%.

(a) What is $17\frac{1}{2}$% of £980?

(b) The total price is £1197.33.
   What is the charge for delivery?

AQA

7 Nick is on holiday in Spain.
He hires a car at the rates shown.

There are 1.60 euros to £1.

Nick hires the car for 5 days and drives
it for a total of 720 kilometres.
Calculate the total cost of hiring the car.
Give your answer in pounds.

CAR HIRE

Daily rate	54 euros
Free kilometres per day	120
Excess kilometre charge	0.60 euros

8 Toffee is sold in bars of two sizes.
A large bar weighs 450 g and costs £1.69. A small bar weighs 275 g and costs 99p.
Which size of bar is better value for money?
You must show all your working.

9 Mrs Tilsed wishes to buy a car priced at £2400.

£2400

Two options are available.
Option 1 – A deposit of 20% of £2400 and 24 monthly payments of £95.
Option 2 – For a single payment the dealer offers a discount of 5% on £2400.

How much more does it cost to buy the car if option 1 is chosen rather than option 2?

10 Terry receives a bill for £284 for repairs to his car. VAT at $17\frac{1}{2}$% is then added to this amount.
Calculate the total amount which Terry pays.

AQA

Personal Finance

- **Hourly pay** is paid at a **basic rate** for a fixed number of hours.
  Overtime pay is usually paid at a higher rate such as time and a half, which means each hour's work is worth 1.5 times the basic rate.

  Eg 1 Alexis is paid £7.20 per hour for a basic 35-hour week.
  Overtime is paid at time and a half.
  Last week she worked 38 hours. How much was Alexis paid last week?

  Basic pay   = £7.20 × 35   = £252
  Overtime pay = 1.5 × £7.20 × 3 = £ 32.40

  Total pay   = £252 + £32.40 = £284.40

- Everyone is allowed to earn some money which is not taxed. This is called a **tax allowance**.

- Tax is only paid on income earned in excess of the tax allowance. This is called **taxable income**.

  Eg 2 Tom earns £5800 per year. His tax allowance is £4615 per year and he pays tax at 10p in the £ on his taxable income. Find how much income tax Tom pays per year.

  Taxable income   = £5800 − £4615 = £1185
  Income tax payable = £1185 × 0.10   = £118.50

  > First find the taxable income, then multiply taxable income by rate in £.

- Gas, electricity and telephone bills are paid **quarterly**.
  The bill consists of a standing charge plus a charge for the amount used.

- You should be able to work out a variety of problems involving personal finance.

Exercise 14

Do not use a calculator for questions 1 to 6.

1. Jenny worked $2\frac{1}{2}$ hours at £5.20 per hour. How much did she earn?

2. Amrit pays his council tax by 10 instalments.
   His first instalment is £143.25 and the other 9 instalments are £137 each.
   How much is his total council tax?

3. Joe insures his house for £90 000 and its contents for £7000.
   The premiums for the insurance are:

   > House: .... 23p per annum for every £100 of cover,
   > Contents: .... £1.30 per annum for every £100 of cover.

   What is the total cost of Joe's insurance?   AQA

4. Last year Harry paid the following gas bills.

   > £146.32   £42.87   £36.55   £133.06

   This year he will pay his gas bills by 12 equal monthly payments.
   Use last year's gas bills to calculate his monthly payments.

5. Kate is paid £6.17 per hour for the 38 hours she has worked in a week.
   Use suitable approximations to estimate Kate's pay for that week.
   You must show all your working.   AQA

6 Karen has an annual income of £5815. She has a tax allowance of £4615.
(a) Calculate Karen's taxable income.

She pays tax at the rate of 10p in the £ on her taxable income.
(b) How much tax does Karen pay per year?

AQA

7 Angela is paid £5.40 per hour for a basic 35-hour week. Overtime is paid at time and a half.
One week Angela worked $37\frac{1}{2}$ hours. How much did Angela earn that week?

8 Steve receives his electricity bill.
The charge for the electricity he has used is £70 plus VAT at 5%.
(a) Calculate the VAT charged.
(b) Hence find the total amount Steve has to pay.

AQA

9 Sharon is a holiday tour representative in Ibiza.
She is paid a basic wage of £600 per month. She also receives a commission of 5% of the cost of the excursions which she sells to her holidaymakers.
In **each** of the 4 weeks of July, she sells £1200 of excursions.
What is Sharon's total pay for July?

AQA

10 Mr. Patel has a faulty shower. He calls out a plumber who replaces some parts costing £8.60.
Copy and complete the bill.

Andy's Plumbers
5 Tapp Street, Bath

	£
Fixed call charge	22.50
1¼ hours at £18 per hour	
Parts	8.60
Total, before VAT	
VAT at 17½%	
Total due	

AQA

11 Francis is paid £6.20 per hour for a basic 35-hour week.
One week Francis also works overtime at time and a half.
His total pay that week was £254.20.
How many hours overtime did he work that week?

12 Leroy earns £13 600 per year.
He has a tax allowance of £4615 and pays tax at the rate of 10p in the £ on the first £1960 of his taxable income and 22p in the £ on the remainder.
How much income tax does he pay each year?

13 An electricity bill is made up of two parts.

> a fixed charge of £9.39, and
> a charge of 6.22p for each unit of electricity used.

VAT at 5% is added to the total.

(a) Hannah uses 743 units of electricity.
Calculate her electricity bill.
(b) Simon receives an electricity bill for £85.21 excluding VAT.
Calculate how many units of electricity Simon has used.

AQA

What you need to know

- The ratio 3 : 2 is read '3 to 2'.

- A ratio is used only to **compare** quantities.
  A ratio does not give information about the exact values of quantities being compared.

- Different forms of the **same ratio**, such as 2 : 1 and 6 : 3, are called **equivalent ratios**.

- In its **simplest form**, a ratio contains whole numbers which have no common factor other than 1.

  | **Eg 1** | Write £2.40 : 40p in its simplest form. |

  £2.40 : 40p = 240p : 40p
  $$= 240 : 40$$
  $$= 6 : 1$$

  > All quantities in a ratio must be in the **same units** before the ratio can be simplified.

- You should be able to solve a variety of problems involving ratio.

  | **Eg 2** | The ratio of bats to balls in a box is 2 : 3.
  There are 12 bats in the box.
  How many balls are there? |

  $12 \div 2 = 6$
  $2 \times 6 : 3 \times 6 = 12 : 18$
  There are 18 balls in the box.

  > For every 2 bats there are 3 balls.
  > To find an equivalent ratio to 2 : 3,
  > in which the first number is 12,
  > multiply each number in the ratio by 6.

  | **Eg 3** | A wall costs £600 to build.
  The costs of materials to labour are in the ratio 1 : 4.
  What is the cost of labour? |

  $1 + 4 = 5$
  £600 ÷ 5 = £120
  Cost of labour = £120 × 4 = £480

  > The numbers in the ratio add to 5.
  > For every £5 of the total cost, £1 pays for materials and £4 pays for labour.
  > So, **divide** by 5 and then **multiply** by 4.

- When two different quantities are always in the **same ratio** the two quantities are in **direct proportion**.

  | **Eg 4** | 20 litres of petrol cost £14.
  Find the cost of 25 litres of petrol. |

  20 litres cost £14
  1 litre costs £14 ÷ 20 = £0.70
  25 litres cost £0.70 × 25 = £17.50

  > This is sometimes called the **unitary method**.
  > **Divide** by 20 to find the cost of 1 litre.
  > **Multiply** by 25 to find the cost of 25 litres.

Exercise 15

Do not use a calculator for questions 1 to 6.

1 Write these ratios in their simplest form.
   (a) 2 : 6   (b) 8 : 4   (c) 6 : 9

2 Rhys draws a plan of his classroom floor. The classroom measures 15 m by 20 m.
   He draws the plan to a scale of 1 cm to 5 m.
   What are the measurements of the classroom floor on the plan?

3 A toy box contains large bricks and small bricks in the ratio 1 : 4.
   The box contains 40 bricks. How many large bricks are in the box?

4 This magnifying glass makes things look larger.
It enlarges in the ratio 1 : 4.

Not to scale

2.4 cm

1.5 cm

(a) How long will the snail look under the magnifying glass?

The moth looks 2.4 cm wide under the magnifying glass.

Not to scale (b) What is the actual width of the moth?

AQA

5 To make mortar a builder mixes sand and cement in the ratio 3 : 1.
The builder uses 2.5 kg of cement. How much sand does he use?

6 In a drama club the ratio of boys to girls is 1 : 3.
(a) What fraction of the club members are boys?
(b) What percentage of the club members are girls?

7 Naheed is given £4. She spends £3.20 and saves the rest.
Express the amount she spends to the amount she saves as a ratio in its simplest form.

8 A pop concert is attended by 2100 people.
The ratio of males to females is 2 : 3.
How many males attended the concert?

9 The ratio of men to women playing golf one day is 5 : 3.
There are 20 men playing. How many women are playing?

10 A town has a population of 45 000 people.
1 in every 180 people are disabled.
How many disabled people are there in the town?

AQA

11 This is a list of ingredients to make
12 rock cakes.
You have plenty of margarine, sugar,
fruit and spice but only 500 g of flour.
What is the largest number of rock cakes
you can make?

Rock cakes (makes 12)
240 g flour   150 g fruit
75 g margarine $\frac{1}{4}$ teaspoon spice
125 g sugar

AQA

12 3 kg of pears cost £2.94. How much will 2 kg of pears cost?

13 Two students are talking about their school outing.

My class went to Tower Bridge last week.
There are 30 people in my class.
The total cost was £172.50

There are 45 people in my group.
What will be the total cost for my group?

14 A Munch Crunch bar weighs 21 g.
The table shows the nutrients that each bar contains.
What is the ratio of protein to carbohydrate?
Give your answer in the form 1 : n.

Protein	1.9 g
Fat	4.7 g
Carbohydrate	13.3 g
Fibre	1.1 g

AQA

What you need to know

- **Speed** is a measurement of how fast something is travelling.
  It involves two other measures, **distance** and **time**.
  In situations where speed is not constant, **average speed** is used.

  $$\text{Speed} = \frac{\text{Distance}}{\text{Time}}$$ $$\text{Average speed} = \frac{\text{Total distance travelled}}{\text{Total time taken}}$$

  The formula linking speed, distance and time can be rearranged and remembered as:
  $$S = D \div T$$
  $$D = S \times T$$
  $$T = D \div S$$

- You should be able to solve problems involving speed, distance and time.

  Eg 1 Wyn takes 2 hours to run 24 km. Calculate his speed in kilometres per hour.

  $$\text{Speed} = \frac{\text{Distance}}{\text{Time}} = \frac{24}{2} = 12 \, \text{km/h}$$

  Eg 2 Norrie says, "If I drive at an average speed of 60 km/h it will take me $2\frac{1}{2}$ hours to complete my journey." What distance is his journey?

  $$\text{Distance} = \text{Speed} \times \text{Time} = 60 \times 2\frac{1}{2} = 150 \, \text{km}$$

  Eg 3 Ellen cycled 15 km at an average speed of 12 km/h. How long did she take?

  $$\text{Time} = \frac{\text{Distance}}{\text{Speed}} = \frac{15}{12} \, \text{hours} = 1\frac{1}{4} \, \text{hours}$$

Exercise 16   Do not use a calculator for questions 1 to 5.

1 Norma travels 128 km in 2 hours. Calculate her average speed in kilometres per hour.

2 Les walked 12 km at an average speed of 4 km/h. How long did he take?

3 Mr Crow took 4 hours to complete a journey. His average speed was 32 miles per hour.
What distance did he travel?

4 A lorry takes $\frac{1}{2}$ hour to travel 20 miles. Calculate the average speed of the lorry in miles per hour.

5 Sean cycled 24 km at an average speed of 16 km/h. How long did he take?

6 Ahmed takes $2\frac{1}{2}$ hours to drive to London. He averages 66 km/h. What distance does he drive?

7 (a) Brian travels 225 miles by train. His journey takes $2\frac{1}{2}$ hours.
What is the average speed of the train?
(b) Val drives 225 miles at an average speed of 50 mph.
How long does her journey take?   AQA

8 Paul takes 15 minutes to run to school. His average running speed is 8 km/h.
How far did he have to run?

9 Lyn cycles 7.2 km in 30 minutes. Calculate her average cycling speed in kilometres per hour?
AQA

10 Shelley drives 205 miles in 4 hours 30 minutes. Calculate her average speed.   AQA

11 Mel cycles home from work, a distance of 5 km.
She leaves work at 1730 and cycles at a steady speed of 15 km per hour.
At what time does she reach home?   AQA

Do not use a calculator for this exercise.

1 (a) Write the number two thousand six hundred and nine in figures.
    (b) Write the number 60 000 000 in words.

2 (a) (i) Write these numbers in order of size, smallest first: 16   10   6   100   61
       (ii) What is the total when the numbers are added together?
    (b) Work out. (i) $100 - 37$ (ii) 100×20 (iii) $100 \div 4$

3 (a) Write the number two thousand and thirty-six in figures.
    (b) Write $\frac{1}{2}$ as a decimal.   (c) Write $\frac{1}{4}$ as a percentage.
    (d) Write the number 638 to the nearest 10.   (e) Write the number 638 to the nearest 100.
                                              AQA

4 Here is a set of numbers: 3, 5, 6, 9, 15, 21.
    (a) Which two of these numbers have a product of 15?
    (b) Which two of these numbers have a difference of 6 **and** a sum of 12?   AQA

5 (a) Work out. (i) $105 - 30$ (ii) 19×7 (iii) $2002 \div 7$
    (b) Work out the square of 14.

6 Orange juice is sold in cartons of two different sizes.

    (a) How much is saved by buying a 500 ml carton instead of two 250 ml cartons?

    (b) Reg buys four 500 ml cartons.
        He pays with a £5 note.
        How much change is he given?

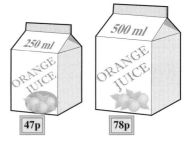

7 The distance from London to Edinburgh via Newcastle is 600 km.
Newcastle is 176 km from Edinburgh. How far is it from London to Newcastle?

8 An overnight train leaves Dundee at 2348 and arrives in London at 0735 the next day.
How long does the journey take? Give your answer in hours and minutes.

9 Kim states that the product of two consecutive whole numbers is an odd number.
By means of an example, show that Kim is **not** correct.   AQA

10 Alison worked for 2 hours 40 minutes and was paid £6 per hour. How much did Alison earn?
                                              AQA

11 Here is a way to multiply a number by 25.

> **STEP 1:** Divide the number by 4
> **STEP 2:** Multiply the answer by 100

    (a) Use **this** way to multiply 84 by 25.
    (b) Explain how you would use your answer to part (a) to work out 85×25.
    (c) How would you change the steps if you wanted a way to **divide** by 25?   AQA

12 (a) 4 litres of milk costs £1.96. How much is 1 litre of milk?
    (b) Apples cost 84 pence per kilogram. What is the cost of 5 kilograms of apples?

13 To buy a car, Ricky has to pay 24 monthly payments of £198.
How much does he have to pay altogether to buy the car?

14 A group of 106 students travel to London by minibuses to watch an international hockey match.
Each minibus can carry 15 passengers. What is the smallest number of minibuses needed?   AQA

15 (a) These diagrams show parts of the number line. Find the number in the middle of each line.

(i) 40 — 70   (ii) 0 — 1 000 000   (iii) −10 — +4

(b) This part of the number line is from 0 to 1.
Copy the number line.
Draw and label arrows to show
where these points are on the line.

0 — 1

(i) $A = 0.1$ (ii) $B = \dfrac{2}{3}$ AQA

16 There are 160 people at a funfair and $\dfrac{1}{4}$ of them are wearing shorts.
How many are wearing shorts?   AQA

17 (a) A supermarket has some special offers.
What is the saving on the orange juice?

Was £1.54 Now 99p

(b) Here are five more special offers.

Marmalade	Oven Chips	Cat Food	Corn Flakes	Tin of Salmon
Was 84p	Was £1.50	Was 58p	Was £1.30	Was £2
Now 64p	Now 80p	Now 29p	Now 80p	Now £1.85

(i)   Which item is now half price?
(ii) On which item do you save the most money?
(iii) Which item has a saving of about one-quarter of the original price?   AQA

18 Clive is making some four-digit numbers. Each number contains all the digits 3, 5, 9 and 6.
(a) Write down the smallest number Clive can make.
(b) Write down the largest **even** number Clive can make.   AQA

19 Samir is baking apple pies and gooseberry pies.
He uses 1.25 kg of flour in the apple pies. He uses 0.92 kg of flour in the gooseberry pies.
How much flour will he have left from a 3 kg bag of flour?   AQA

20 A ski-run measures 7.5 cm on a map. The map is drawn to a scale of 1 cm to 200 m.
What is the actual length of the ski-run in metres?

21 How much will it cost to hire a trailer for 5 days?

TRAILERS FOR HIRE
£3.50 per day
plus £12.50 insurance

22 A sports club is given £100 to spend on
new footballs. A new football costs £7.99.
What is the greatest number of footballs they can buy?

23 (a) Calculate the cost per litre of emulsion paint,
correct to the nearest penny.
(b) How much more does it cost to buy
10 litres of gloss paint than
10 litres of emulsion paint?

GLOSS PAINT 5 litres £12.95
EMULSION PAINT 10 litres £14.99

24 Write 0.7 as a fraction.

25 (a) Write 34.849 correct to one decimal place.   (b) Work out $4.7 - 2.81$ AQA

26 A crowd of 54 000 people watch a carnival.
(a) 15% of the crowd are men. How many men watch the carnival?
(b) Two-thirds of the crowd are children. How many children watch the carnival?

27 Sonia is paid a basic rate of £4.80 per hour for working a 30-hour week from Monday to Friday.
  (a) How much is Sonia paid each week?

  When Sonia works on a Saturday she is paid at time and a half.
  (b) How much is Sonia paid for 1 hour's work on a Saturday?
  (c) For working last Saturday Sonia was paid £21.60.
       How many hours did she work last Saturday?

28 The temperature at 6 am is $-3°C$. The temperature at 6 pm is 5°C.
  How many degrees warmer is it at 6 pm than at 6 am?

29 One dollar is worth about 62 pence. Mr Jones buys a watch that costs 89 dollars.
  Estimate how much the watch is worth in pounds.   AQA

30 (a) (i)   What is the value of the 3 in the number 2439?
       (ii) What is the value of the 3 in the answer to 2439×100?
  (b) Work out. (i) $8 - 3 \times 2$ (ii) $15 \div (3 + 2) - 1$
  (c) Work out. (i) $600 - 147$ (ii) 137×32 (iii) $432 \div 12$

31 (a) Work out. (i) 10^5 (ii) $10^2 - 2^3$ (iii) $2^3 \times 3^2$ (iv) $30^2 \div 10^3$
  (b) Which is smaller, 5^2 or 3^3? Show **all** your working.

32 Jake cycles 24 km at 16 km/h. He sets off at 0945. At what time does he finish?

33 Gavin wins £48.
  He gives his son one quarter of his winnings. He gives half of the remainder to his wife.
  What fraction of his winnings does he keep for himself?

34 A plank of wood is 225 cm in length. It is cut into two pieces.
  One piece is 37 cm longer than the other. What is the length of the shorter piece of wood? AQA

35 Luxury Limos has 79 company cars. In one week, these cars have been driven a
  total of 76 219 miles.
  (a) Which two numbers would you use to find a quick **estimate** of how far each car has
       been driven?

  The manager looks at the figures and states that each car has only been driven 100 miles
  on average.
  (b) Is the manager's estimate correct? Use your answer to part (a) to support your answer. AQA

36 (a) A postwoman has only 1st class and 2nd class letters in her post bag.
       80% of the letters are 1st class.
       There are 320 letters altogether. How many letters are 1st class?
  (b) A mail van has 9000 letters and 150 parcels.
       Express the number of letters to the number of parcels as a ratio in its simplest form. AQA

37 A train travels from Basingstoke to London in 40 minutes. The distance is 50 miles.
  Find the average speed of the train in miles per hour.   AQA

38 A quiz has 40 questions.
  (a) Grace gets 65% of the questions right.
       How many questions did she get right?
  (b) Lenny gets 34 questions right.
       What percentage of the questions did he get right?

39 (a) Estimate $\dfrac{53 \times 197}{3.9}$ (b) Work out. (i) $1\frac{1}{4} + \frac{2}{3}$ (ii) $\frac{2}{3} - \frac{1}{4}$

40 A packet contains 12 fibre-tipped pens.
  Henry and Alice share them in the ratio 1 : 3.
  How many does Alice receive?   AQA

You may use a calculator for this exercise.

1 (a) Which of the numbers 8, −4, 0 or 5 is an odd number?
   (b) Write the number 3568 to the nearest 10.
   (c) What is the value of the 4 in the number 3.42?

2 (a) List these numbers in order, smallest first.

   | 13 | 5 | −7 | 0 | −1 |

   (b) What is the difference between the largest number and the smallest number in your list?

3 Giles buys a newspaper for 55p and a computer magazine for £2.10.
   What change will he get from a £5 note?

4 Isaac buys 180 grams of sweets from the Pic 'n' Mix selection.
   The price of the sweets is 65p per 100 g.
   How much does he have to pay?

5 In a long jump event Hanniah jumped the following distances.
   5.15 m   4.95 m   5.20 m   5.02 m   5.10 m
   (a) Write down the shortest distance Hanniah jumped.
   (b) Write these distances in order, shortest first.

6 Some of the rail services from Poole to Waterloo are shown.

Poole	0544	0602	—	0640	—	0740	0825	0846
Bournemouth	0558	0616	—	0654	0715	0754	0839	0900
Southampton	0634	0655	0714	0738	0754	0838	0908	0938
Eastleigh	0646	—	—	0750	—	0852	—	0951
Waterloo	0804	0810	0844	0901	0908	1005	1018	1112

   (a) Sid arrives at Bournemouth station at 0830.
       What is the time of the next train to Eastleigh?
   (b) Paul catches the 0654 from Bournemouth to Southampton.
       How many minutes does the journey take?

7 Eric earns £491 per month. He has a tax allowance of £4615 per year.
   (a) How much is Eric's taxable income per year?

   He pays tax at the rate of 10p in the pound.
   (b) How much tax does Eric pay per year?   AQA

8 A quiz consists of ten questions. Beth, John and Sue take part.
   These are their results.

   A correct answer scores 3 points.
   An incorrect answer scores −2 points.
   A question not attempted scores 0 points.

	Beth	John	Sue
Number of answers correct	4	6	5
Number of answers incorrect	4	3	1
Number of questions not attempted	2	1	4

   Who scores the most points? Show your working.   AQA

9 Bruce buys two packets of baby wipes on special offer.
   Calculate the actual cost of
   each baby wipe.

   40 BABY WIPES
   £2.24

   Special Offer
   **BUY ONE
   GET ONE FREE**

10 (a) Write $\frac{7}{9}$ as a decimal. Give your answer correct to two decimal places.

(b) Write 33%, 0.3, $\frac{8}{25}$ and $\frac{1}{3}$ in order of size, smallest first.

11 Cheri is paid a basic rate of £5.40 per hour for a 35-hour week.

Overtime is paid at $1\frac{1}{2}$ times the basic rate.

Last week she worked 41 hours. Calculate her pay for last week.

12 On a musical keyboard there are 5 black keys for every 7 white keys.
The keyboard has 28 white keys. How many black keys does it have?

13 Work out. (a) $6.25 \times 13 - 6.25 \times 3$ (b) $\frac{2}{5}$ of 12 (c) $3.5^2 - 2.5^2$

14 A packet of washing powder costs £3.96 and weighs 1.5 kg.
The packet has enough powder for 22 washes.
(a) What is the cost of powder for one wash?
(b) How much powder is needed for one wash?
Give your answer in grams correct to one decimal place.

AQA

15 (a) Write down a decimal that lies halfway between 0.4 and 0.5.
(b) A turkey costs £2.40 per kilogram.
What is the cost of a turkey which weighs 6.5 kilograms?

16 (a) James earns £9650 a year. He gets a pay rise of 6%.
(i) How much **more** does James earn after the pay rise?
(ii) What is James' new pay per year?

(b) Frances is paid £11 400 a year. She takes home $\frac{4}{5}$ of her pay.

(i) How much does Frances take home each year?
(ii) Frances is paid monthly. How much does she take home each month?

AQA

17 (a) Write these fractions in ascending order: $\frac{1}{2}$ $\frac{2}{3}$ $\frac{3}{5}$ $\frac{5}{8}$ $\frac{3}{4}$

(b) Write down a fraction that lies halfway between $\frac{1}{5}$ and $\frac{1}{4}$.

(c) Work out. (i) $\frac{1}{4} + \frac{2}{5}$ (ii) $\frac{4}{5} \times \frac{1}{2}$

18 Jacob is 3.7 kg heavier than Isaac. The sum of their weights is 44.5 kg. How heavy is Jacob?

19 In America a camera cost $110.
In England an identical camera costs £65.
The exchange rate is £1 = $1.62
In which country is the camera cheaper and by how much?
You must show all your working.

$110   £65

AQA

20 (a) Write $\frac{13}{20}$ as a decimal.

(b) In a spelling test Lara scores 13 out of 20. What is Lara's score as a percentage?

21 (a) Given that $576 \times 135 = 77\,760$, find (i) 57.6×13.5, (ii) $\frac{7776}{5760}$.
(b) Write 77 760 correct to one significant figure.

22 A shop sells 4000 items in a week. 5% are returned.

$\frac{1}{4}$ of the returned items are faulty. How many items are faulty?

AQA

23 A car takes $2\frac{1}{2}$ hours to travel 150 km.

Calculate the average speed of the car in kilometres per hour.

24 Bertie has to work out $4.2 \times 4.9 \times 31$. He uses a calculator and gets 6379.8
(a) By rounding each number to one significant figure check Bertie's answer.
Show all your working.
(b) What is the mistake in Bertie's answer?

25 Colin buys two cups of tea and three cups of coffee. He pays £4.65 altogether.
The price of a cup of tea is 84 pence. What is the price of a cup of coffee? AQA

26 The cost of 6 medium eggs is 48 pence.
(a) How much will 10 medium eggs cost?
(b) Small eggs cost $\frac{7}{8}$ of the price of medium eggs. How much will 6 small eggs cost?
(c) Large eggs cost 25% more than medium eggs. How much will 6 large eggs cost? AQA

27 The size and selling price of small and medium toothpaste is shown.

TOOTHPASTE **Small Size 72 ml 50p**

TOOTHPASTE **Medium Size 135 ml 98p**

Which size of toothpaste gives better value for money?
You **must** show all your working. AQA

28 Tom buys 200 tomato plants at a total cost of £40 to sell at a school fair.
He sells $\frac{3}{4}$ of them at 50p each.
He then reduces the price of the remaining plants by 20%.
(a) Calculate the new price of a tomato plant.
(b) At the end of the day there are 18 plants left which have not been sold.
How much money does he receive from selling the plants at the school fair? AQA

29 To make squash, orange juice and water is mixed in the ratio of 1 : 6.
How much orange juice is needed to make 3.5 litres of squash?

30 Mrs Joy's electricity meter was read on 1st March and 1st June.
On 1st March the reading was 3 2 4 5 7 On 1st June the reading was 3 2 9 3 1
(a) How many units of electricity have been used?

Her electricity bill for this period includes a fixed charge of £9.58 and the cost of the units used at 6.36 pence per unit.
(b) Calculate the total cost of electricity for this period.

31 Four cabbages cost £2.88. How much will five cabbages cost? AQA

32 Petrol costs 78.9 pence per litre. A car can travel 8.5 miles on one litre of petrol.
Calculate the cost of travelling 1000 miles in the car.
Give your answer to a suitable degree of accuracy. AQA

33 Ruby buys a new exhaust for her car. The cost is £98 plus $17\frac{1}{2}\%$ VAT.
How much does she have to pay altogether?

34 Tom lives 2 kilometres from work.
He walks to work at an average speed of 5 km/h.
He leaves home at 0845. At what time does he arrive at work? AQA

35 A caravan is for sale at £7200. Stuart buys the caravan on credit.

The credit terms are: deposit 25% of sale price and 36 monthly payments of £175.

Express the extra amount paid for credit, compared with the cash price,
as a percentage of the cash price.

FOR SALE
£7200

43

What you need to know

- **Multiples** of a number are found by multiplying the number by 1, 2, 3, 4, …
  Eg 1 The multiples of 8 are $1 \times 8 = 8$, $2 \times 8 = 16$, $3 \times 8 = 24$, $4 \times 8 = 32$, …

- **Factors** of a number are found by listing all the products that give the number.
  Eg 2 $1 \times 6 = 6$ and $2 \times 3 = 6$. So, the factors of 6 are: 1, 2, 3 and 6.

- The **common factors** of two numbers are the numbers which are factors of **both**.
  Eg 3 Factors of 16 are: 1, 2, 4, 8, 16.   Factors of 24 are: 1, 2, 3, 4, 6, 8, 12, 24.
  Common factors of 16 and 24 are: 1, 2, 4, 8.

- You should be able to find the **squares** and **cubes** of numbers.

- Be able to find the square root of a number.
  Eg 4 The positive square root of 9 is 3.   This can be written as $\sqrt{9} = 3$.

- Be able to find the reciprocal of a number.
  The **reciprocal** of a number is the value obtained when the number is divided into 1.
  Eg 5 The reciprocal of 2 is given by $1 \div 2 = \dfrac{1}{2}$.

- Be able to use the $\boxed{x^2}$, $\boxed{x^y}$, $\boxed{\sqrt{}}$ and $\boxed{\frac{1}{x}}$ buttons on a calculator to solve a variety of problems.

Exercise 17

Do not use a calculator for questions 1 to 7.

1 Look at these numbers: 2   5   8   11   14   17   20
   (a)   Which of these numbers are factors of 10?
   (b)   Which of these numbers is a multiple of 10?

2 (a) $24 = 3 \times 8$ or $24 = 8 \times 3$
      Write down two other multiplications for which the answer is 24.
   (b)   Write down **all** the factors of 24.
   (c)   Copy and fill in the missing numbers in this factor tree.

   AQA

3 (a)   Write down a multiple of 7 between 30 and 40.
   (b)   Write down all the factors of 18.
   (c)   Find the common factors of 18 and 24.

4 A number of counters can be grouped into 2's, 3's and 4's.
   Find the smallest possible number of counters.

5 What is   (a)   the square of 4,   (b)   the square root of 81,   (c)   the reciprocal of 4?

6 (a)   Work out the value of   (i) 5^3 (ii) $\sqrt{64}$
   (b)   Between which two consecutive whole numbers does $\sqrt{30}$ lie?   AQA

7 (a)   **Without using a calculator**, write down an estimate of the square root of 40.
      Give your estimate correct to one decimal place and show your working.   AQA

8 (a)   Find the reciprocal of 7. Give your answer correct to two decimal places.
   (b)   Calculate.   (i) $3.4 - \dfrac{1}{1.6}$ (ii) $\sqrt{7.29}$ (iii) $2.4^2 \times \sqrt{1.44}$

What you need to know

- You should be able to write **algebraic expressions**.

  Eg 1 An expression for the cost of 6 pens at n pence each is $6n$ pence.

- Be able to **simplify expressions** by collecting **like terms** together.

  Eg 2 (a) $2d + 3d = 5d$ (b) $3x + 2 - x + 4 = 2x + 6$ (c) $x + 2x + x^2 = 3x + x^2$

- Be able to **multiply expressions** together.

  Eg 3 (a) $2 \times a \times a = 2a^2$ (b) $y \times y \times y = y^3$ (c) $m \times 3n = 3mn$

- Be able to **multiply out brackets**.

  Eg 4 (a) $2(x + 5) = 2x + 10$ (b) $x(x - 5) = x^2 - 5x$

- Be able to **factorise expressions**.

  Eg 5 (a) $3x - 6 = 3(x - 2)$ (b) $m^2 + 5m = m(m + 5)$

Exercise 18

1 A calculator costs £9. Write an expression for the cost of k calculators.

2 Godfrey is 5 years older than Mary.
Write an expression for Godfrey's age when Mary is t years old.

3 A cup of coffee costs x pence and a cup of tea costs y pence.
Write an expression for the cost of 3 cups of coffee and 2 cups of tea.

4 Write an expression, in terms of x,
for the sum of the angles in this shape.

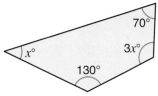

5 A muffin costs $d + 3$ pence. Write an expression for the cost of 5 muffins.

6 Simplify the expressions.   (a) $2p + p + 5p$ (b) $t \times t \times t$ (c) $5x + y - 2x + 3y$

            AQA

7 Which algebraic expressions are equivalent?

$2y$	y^2	$2(y + 1)$	$y \times y$	$y + y$
$2y + 2$	$2y + y$	$2y^2$	$3y$	$2y + 1$

            AQA

8 (a) Simplify   (i) $2x + 3 + x$,   (ii) $2x + y - x + y$.
    (b) Multiply out   (i) $2(x + 3)$,   (ii) $x(x - 1)$.
    (c) Multiply out and simplify   (i) $2(x - 1) - 3$,   (ii) $7 + 3(2 + x)$.
    (d) Factorise   (i) $2a - 6$,   (ii) $x^2 + 2x$.

9 (a) Simplify $9p + 4q + 6p - 7q$.
    (b) Multiply out and simplify $8(x + 3) + 5(2x + 4)$.

            AQA

Solving Equations

What you need to know

- The solution of an equation is the value of the unknown letter that fits the equation.

- You should be able to solve simple equations by **inspection**.

  Eg 1 (a) $a + 2 = 5$ (b) $m - 3 = 7$ (c) $2x = 10$
            $a = 3$ $m = 10$ $x = 5$

- Be able to solve simple problems by **working backwards**.

  Eg 2 I think of a number, multiply it by 3 and add 4. The answer is 19.

  The number I thought of is 5.

- Be able to use the **balance method** to solve equations.

  Eg 3 Solve these equations.

  (a) $d - 13 = -5$ (b) $-4a = 20$ (c) $5 - 4n = -1$

         $d = -5 + 13$ $a = \dfrac{20}{-4}$ $-4n = -6$

         $d = 8$ $a = -5$ $n = 1.5$

Exercise 19

1 What number should be put in the box to make each of these statements correct?

(a) $\square - 6 = 9$ (b) $2 + \square = 11$ (c) $4 \times \square = 20$ (d) $\square \times 3 - 5 = 7$

2 Solve these equations.

(a) $7 + x = 12$ (b) $5 - x = 3$ (c) $3x = 21$ (d) $2x - 1 = 5$

3

Teacher: Think of a number, double it and add 5.

Zeenat: The number I thought of was 25.

John: My answer was 19.

(a) What answer did Zeenat get?

(b) What was the number John thought of?

                                             AQA

4 (a) I think of a number, add 3, and then multiply by 2.
The answer is 16. What is my number?

(b) I think of a number, double it and then subtract 3.
The answer is 5. What is my number?

5 Solve these equations.

(a) $3x - 7 = 23$ (b) $4 + 3x = 19$ (c) $5x - 9 = 11$ (d) $5 - 7x = 47$

6 Solve these equations.

(a) $3x + 5 = 2$ (b) $4x = 2$ (c) $4x + 1 = 23$ (d) $5x + 1 = -3$

Further Equations

What you need to know

- To solve an equation you need to find the numerical value of the letter, by ending up with **one letter** on one side of the equation and a **number** on the other side of the equation.

- You should be able to solve equations with unknowns on both sides of the equals sign.

  Eg 1 Solve $3x + 1 = x + 7$.
  $$3x = x + 6$$
  $$2x = 6$$
  $$x = 3$$

- Be able to solve equations which include brackets.

  Eg 2 Solve $2(x - 3) = 4$.
  $$2x - 6 = 4$$
  $$2x = 10$$
  $$x = 5$$

- You should be able to write, or form, equations using the information given in a problem.

Exercise 20

1 Solve the equations (a) $3x - 7 = x + 15$, (b) $5(x - 2) = 20$.

2 Solve these equations.
   (a) $7x + 4 = 60$ (b) $3x - 7 = -4$ (c) $2(x + 3) = -2$ (d) $3x - 4 = 1 + x$

3 Solve the equations (a) $2x + 3 = 15$, (b) $3(x - 1) = 6$, (c) $x + 2 = 5 - x$.
   AQA

4 Solve these equations.
   (a) $2x + 5 = 2$ (b) $2(x - 1) = 3$ (c) $5 - 2x = 3x + 2$ (d) $2(3 + x) = 9$

5 Solve the equation $7y - 1 = 3 - y$.
   AQA

6 The lengths of these rods are given, in centimetres, in terms of n.

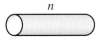 n 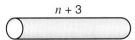 $n + 3$ $2n - 1$

   (a) Write an expression, in terms of n, for the total length of the rods.
   (b) The total length of the rods is $30\,\text{cm}$.
       By forming an equation, find the value of n.

7 Mandy buys a small box of chocolates and a large box of chocolates.
   The diagram shows the number of chocolates in each box.

   Altogether there are 47 chocolates.
   By forming an equation, find the number
   of chocolates in the larger box.

n
chocolates

$2n + 5$
chocolates

8 Solve the equation $4(3 - x) = 20$.

9 Solve these equations. (a) $3x - 5 = 16$ (b) $7x + 1 = 2x + 4$

10 Solve the equation $5(x - 3) = 2x$.

What you need to know

- An **expression** is just an answer using letters and numbers.
  A **formula** is an algebraic rule. It always has an equals sign.

- You should be able to **write simple formulae**.

  Eg 1 A packet of crisps weighs 25 grams.
  Write a formula for the total weight,
  W grams, of n packets of crisps.
  $$W = 25n$$

  Eg 2 Start with t, add 5 and then multiply
  by 3. The result is p.
  Write a formula for p in terms of t.
  $$p = 3(t + 5)$$

- Be able to **substitute** values into given expressions and formulae.

  Eg 3 (a) Find the value
  of $4x - y$ when
  $x = 5$ and $y = 7$.
  $$4x - y = 4 \times 5 - 7$$
  $$= 20 - 7$$
  $$= 13$$

  (b) $A = pq - r$
  Find the value
  of A when $p = 2$,
  $q = -2$ and $r = 3$.
  $$A = pq - r$$
  $$= 2 \times (-2) - 3$$
  $$= -4 - 3$$
  $$= -7$$

  (c) $M = 2n^2$
  Find the value
  of M when $n = 3$.
  $$M = 2n^2$$
  $$= 2 \times 3^2$$
  $$= 2 \times 9$$
  $$= 18$$

Exercise 21

Do not use a calculator for questions 1 to 8.

1 What is the value of $a - 3b$ when $a = 10$ and $b = 2$?

2 What is the value of $2x + y$ when $x = -3$ and $y = 5$?

3 (a) Work out $4p - 1$ when $p = 10$.
(b) Work out $8a + 4b$ when (i) $a = 2$ and $b = 3$, (ii) $a = 2$ and $b = -3$. AQA

4 $H = ab - c$. Find the value of H when $a = 2$, $b = -5$ and $c = 3$.

5 A boat is hired. The cost, in £, is given by: | Cost = 6 × Number of hours + 5 |

(a) Calculate the cost of hiring the boat for 2 hours.
(b) The boat was hired at a cost of £29. For how many hours was it hired? AQA

6 $L = 5(p + q)$. Find the value of L when $p = 2$ and $q = -4$.

7 $A = b - cd$. Find the value of A when $b = -3$, $c = 2$ and $d = 4$.

8 What is the value of $10y^2$ when $y = 3$?

9 Using $p = 18.8$, $q = 37.2$, $r = 0.4$, work out: (a) $p + \dfrac{q}{r}$ (b) $\dfrac{p + q}{r}$ AQA

10 This rule is used to change miles into kilometres.

| Multiply the number of miles by 8 and then divide by 5 |

(a) Use the rule to change 25 miles into kilometres.
(b) Using K for the number of kilometres and M for the number of miles write a formula for K in terms of M.
(c) Use your formula to find the value of M when $K = 60$.

Sequences ●●●●●●●●●●●●●●

What you need to know

● A **sequence** is a list of numbers made according to some rule.
The numbers in a sequence are called **terms**.

● You should be able to draw and continue number sequences represented by patterns of shapes.

Eg 1   This pattern represents the sequence:
3, 5, 7, …

● Be able to continue a sequence by following a given rule.

Eg 2   The sequence   2, 7, 22, …   is made using the rule:

> multiply the last number by 3, then add 1.

The next term in the sequence = $(22 \times 3) + 1 = 66 + 1 = 67$

● Be able to find a rule, and then use it, to continue a sequence.

> **To continue a sequence:**
> 1. Work out the rule to get from one term to the next.
> 2. Apply the same rule to find further terms in the sequence.

Eg 3   Describe the rule used to make the following sequences.
Then use the rule to find the next term of each sequence.

(a) 5, 8, 11, 14, …   (b) 2, 4, 8, 16, …   (c) 1, 1, 2, 3, 5, 8, …
Rule: Rule: Rule:
add 3 to last term   multiply last term by 2   add the last two terms
Next term: 17   Next term: 32   Next term: 13

> **Special sequences - Square numbers:**   1, 4, 9, 16, 25, …
> **Triangular numbers:**   1, 3, 6, 10, 15, …

Exercise 22

1   Write down the next two terms in each of these sequences.
(a) 1, 5, 9, 13, 17, …   (b) 50, 46, 42, 38, 34, ….

2   Sasha makes a sequence of patterns with sticks. Here are his first three patterns.

Pattern 1   **Pattern 2**   **Pattern 3**

(a)   Draw Pattern 4.
(b)   Copy and complete the table.

Pattern number	1	2	3	4
Number of sticks	3	5		

(c)   How many sticks will Sasha use for Pattern 5?
(d)   There are 33 sticks in Pattern 16.
How many sticks are in Pattern 17?

AQA

3 The first three patterns in a sequence are shown.

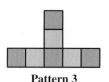

Pattern 1   **Pattern 2**   **Pattern 3**

(a) Draw Pattern 4.
(b) How many squares are in Pattern 5?
     Explain how you found your answer.
(c) There are 58 squares in Pattern 20.
     How many squares are in Pattern 19?

4 What is the next number in each of these sequences?

(a) 1, 2, 5, 10, …   (b) 1, 3, 9, 27, …   (c) 1, $\frac{1}{2}$, $\frac{1}{4}$, $\frac{1}{8}$, …

5 Part of a number sequence is: …, 11, 15, 19, 23, …
(a) Write down the number which comes after 23 in the sequence.
(b) Write down the number which comes before 11 in the sequence.
(c) Write down the rule for making this sequence.   AQA

6 Look at this sequence of numbers. 2, 5, 8, 11, ….
(a) What is the next number in the sequence?
(b) Is 30 a number in this sequence?
     Give a reason for your answer.

7 The rule for a sequence is:

> Add the last two numbers and divide by 2.

Write down the next three terms when the sequence begins: 3, 7, …

8 A sequence begins: 5, 15, 45, 135, ….
(a) Write down the rule, in words, used to get from one term to the next in the sequence.
(b) Use your rule to find the next term in the sequence.

9 A sequence begins: 1, −2, …
The next number in the sequence is found by using the rule:

> ADD THE PREVIOUS TWO NUMBERS AND MULTIPLY BY TWO

Use the rule to find the next **two** numbers in the sequence.   AQA

10 Ahmed writes down the first four numbers of a sequence: 10, 8, 4, −2, …
(a) What is the next number in this sequence?
(b) Explain how you found your answer.   AQA

11 The first six terms of a sequence are shown. 1, 4, 5, 9, 14, 23, ….
Write down the next two terms.

12 A sequence begins: 1, 6, 10, 8, ….
The rule to continue the sequence is:
double the difference between the last two numbers.
Ravi says if you continue the sequence it will end in 0. Is he correct?
Explain your answer.

13 (a) Write down the first **three** terms of the sequence whose nth term is given by $n^2 + 4$.
(b) Will the number 106 be in this sequence?
     Explain your answer.   AQA

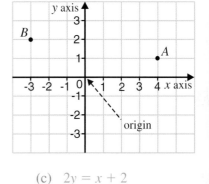

What you need to know

- **Coordinates** (involving positive and negative numbers) are used to describe the position of a point on a graph.

  Eg 1 The coordinates of A are $(4, 1)$.
  The coordinates of B are $(-3, 2)$.

- The x axis is the line $y = 0$. The y axis is the line $x = 0$.

- The x axis crosses the y axis at the **origin**.

- You should be able to draw the graph of a straight line.

  Eg 2 Draw the graphs of the following lines.

  (a) $y = 2$ (b) $x = 3$ (c) $2y = x + 2$

The graph is a **horizontal** line. All points on the line have y coordinate 2.	The graph is a **vertical** line. All points on the line have x coordinate 3.	Find values for x and y.

Find values for x and y.

x	0	2	4
y	1	2	3

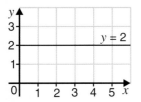 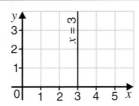 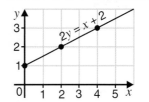

- Be able to draw the graph of a straight line by finding the points where the line crosses the x axis and the y axis.

  Eg 3 Draw the graph of the line $x + 2y = 4$.

  To find the x coordinate of the point where a line crosses the x axis, substitute $y = 0$ into the equation of the line.

  When $y = 0$, $x + 0 = 4$, $x = 4$. Plot $(4, 0)$.

  To find the y coordinate of the point where a line crosses the y axis, substitute $x = 0$ into the equation of the line.

  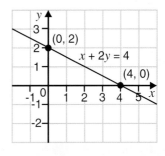

  When $x = 0$, $0 + 2y = 4$, $y = 2$. Plot $(0, 2)$.

  A straight line drawn through the points $(0, 2)$ and $(4, 0)$ is the graph of $x + 2y = 4$.

Exercise 23

1 The line joining points P and Q is shown.

(a) Write down the coordinates of points P and Q.

(b) Find the coordinates of the midpoint of the line PQ.

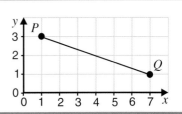

23

2 Points R and S are shown.

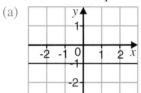

(a) Write down the coordinates of points R and S.
(b) The straight line joining R and S crosses the x axis at T.
Write down the coordinates of T.

3 Draw and label x and y axes from -5 to 4.
(a) On your diagram plot $A(4, 3)$ and $B(-5, -3)$.
(b) $C(p, -1)$ is on the line segment AB.
What is the value of p?

4 (a) On the same diagram draw the lines $y = 2$ and $x = 5$.
(b) Write down the coordinates of the point where the lines cross.

5 Write down the equations of the lines drawn on these diagrams.

(a)

(b)

(c)

6 (a) Copy and complete the table of values for $y = 1 - 2x$.
(b) Draw the line $y = 1 - 2x$ for values of x from -3 to 3.
(c) Use your graph to find the value of y when $x = -1.5$.

x	-3	0	3
y		1	

7 On the same diagram, draw and label the lines: $y = x + 1$ and $y = 1 - x$.   AQA

8 On separate diagrams draw the graphs of each of these equations for values of x from -2 to 2.
(a) $y = 2x$ (b) $y - x = 2$ (c) $y + x = 2$ (d) $2y = x$

9 (a) Copy and complete the table of values for $2y = 3x - 6$.
(b) Draw the graph of $2y = 3x - 6$
for values of x from -2 to 4.
(c) Use your graph to find the value of x when $y = 1.5$.

x	-2	0	4
y		-3	

10 (a) Copy and complete the table of values for the equation $5y - 2x = 10$.
(b) Draw the graph of $5y - 2x = 10$
for values of x from -5 to 5.
Label the x axis from -5 to 5 and the y axis from 0 to 4.
(c) Use your graph to find the value of y when $x = -2$.

x	0		5
y		0	

11 (a) On the same diagram, draw and label the lines $y = x - 1$ and $x + y = 5$
for values of x from 0 to 5.
(b) Write down the coordinates of the point where the lines cross.

What you need to know

● A graph used to change from one quantity into an equivalent quantity is called a **conversion graph**.

Eg 1 Use 15 kilograms = 33 pounds (lb) to draw a conversion graph for kilograms and pounds.

Use your graph to find (a) 5 kilograms in pounds, (b) 20 pounds in kilograms.

The straight line drawn through the points (0, 0) and (33, 15) is the conversion graph for kilograms and pounds.

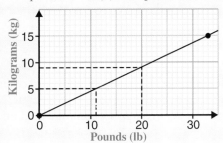

Reading from the graph:
(a) 5 kg = 11 lb
(b) 20 lb = 9 kg

● **Distance-time graphs** are used to illustrate journeys.

On a distance-time graph:
Speed can be calculated from the gradient of a line.
The faster the speed the steeper the gradient.
Zero gradient (horizontal line) means zero speed.

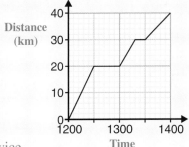

Eg 2 The graph shows a car journey.
(a) How many times does the car stop?
(b) (i) Between what times does the car travel fastest? Explain your answer.
(ii) What is the speed of the car during this part of the journey?

(a) Twice
(b) (i) 1200 to 1230. Steepest gradient.
(ii) Speed = $\dfrac{\text{Distance}}{\text{Time}} = \dfrac{20\,\text{km}}{\frac{1}{2}\,\text{hour}} = 40\,\text{km/h}$

● You should be able to draw and interpret graphs arising from real-life situations.

Exercise 24

1 This graph can be used to convert miles to kilometres.

(a) Scott lives $3\frac{1}{2}$ miles from the Post Office. How many kilometres is this?

(b) Jade goes for a training run of 7 kilometres. How many miles is this?

(c) Jade is training to run a half marathon, which is a distance of 13 miles. Use the graph to calculate this distance in kilometres.

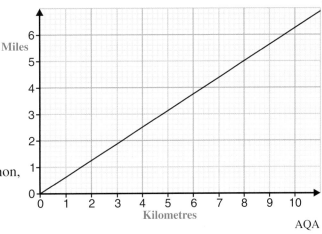

AQA

24

2 The distance by boat from Poole Quay to Wareham is 12 miles.
The distance-time graph shows a boat trip from Poole Quay to Wareham and back.

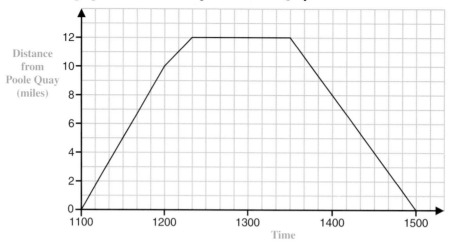

(a) Describe what happened to the speed of the boat at 1200 hours.
(b) How long did the boat stay in Wareham?
(c) What was the average speed of the boat on the return journey from Wareham to Poole Quay?

AQA

3 Ken drives from his home to the city centre.
The graph represents his journey.

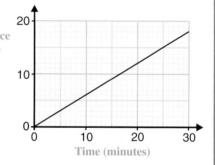

(a) How long did Ken take to reach the city centre?

(b) How far from the city centre does Ken live?

(c) What is his average speed for the journey in kilometres per hour?

4 The table shows the largest quantity of salt, w grams, which can be dissolved in a beaker of water at temperature t°C.

(a) Draw a graph to illustrate this information.

t°C	10	20	25	30	40	50	60
w grams	54	58	60	62	66	70	74

(b) Use your graph to find
  (i) the lowest temperature at which 63 g of salt will dissolve in the water,
  (ii) the largest amount of salt that will dissolve in the water at 44°C.

AQA

5 (a) Given that 7.4 square metres = 80 square feet, draw a conversion graph for square metres to square feet.

(b) Use your graph to change
  (i) 5 square metres into square feet, (ii) 32 square feet into square metres.

6 The graph shows the temperature of the water in a tank as it is being heated.

(a) What was the temperature of the water before it was heated?

(b) How long did it take for the water to reach 26°C?

(c) Estimate the number of minutes it will take for the temperature of the water to rise from 32°C to 50°C.

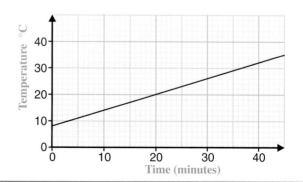

Section Review - Number and Algebra

1 Copy the diagram.

  (a) What are the coordinates of A?

  (b) Plot the point $B(2, 3)$.

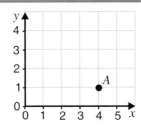

2 A sequence begins   2,   4,   6,   …

To continue the sequence use the rule: Add 2 to the last term.

  (a) Write down the next term in the sequence.

  (b) Explain why the number 99 is not a term in this sequence.

3 In each part, find the output when the input is 12.

  (a)

  (b)

4 Use this rule to find the number of points a football team has scored.

Points scored = $3 \times$ Number of wins + Number of draws

A team wins 7 games and draws 5. How many points have they scored?

5 Regular pentagons are used to form patterns, as shown.

  (a) Draw Pattern 4.

  (b) Copy and complete the table.

Pattern number	1	2	3	4
Number of sides	5	8	11	

Pattern 1   **Pattern 2**   **Pattern 3**

  (c) How many sides has Pattern 5?

  (d) Pattern 10 has 32 sides. How many sides has Pattern 11?

6 Find the value of $3a + 2b$ when $a = 5$ and $b = 3$.

7 (a) A list of numbers is given.   4   5   6   12   24   36   45

  (i) Which of these numbers is a factor of 18?

  (ii) Which of these numbers is a multiple of 8?

  (b) What are the common factors of 24 and 36?

8 Donna and Todd work at SupaMotors selling cars.

Their weekly pay is calculated using this formula: Pay = £20 for each car sold plus £75.

  (a) Donna sells 5 cars in one week. Work out her pay for this week.

  (b) Last week Todd's pay was £215. How many cars did he sell last week?   AQA

9 (a) On graph paper, plot the points $A(-3, -2)$ and $B(1, 4)$.

  (b) What are the coordinates of the midpoint of AB?

10 A jam doughnut costs t pence.

  (a) Write an expression for the cost of 5 jam doughnuts.

A cream doughnut costs 5 pence more than a jam doughnut.

  (b) Write an expression for the cost of a cream doughnut.

11 What number should be put in the box to make each of these statements correct?

  (a) $\boxed{} - 3 = 7$ (b) $\boxed{} + 5 = 9$ (c) $3 \times \boxed{} = 6$

12 Which is smaller $\sqrt{64}$ or 3^2? Show your working.

13 (a) (i) What is the next term in this sequence? 2, 9, 16, 23, …
   (ii) Will the 50th term in the sequence be an odd number or an even number?
       Give a reason for your answer.
   (b) Another sequence begins 1, 5, 9, 13, 17, …
       Describe in words the rule for continuing the sequence.

14 $2n$ represents any even number.
   Which of the statements describes the number   (a) n,   (b) $2n + 1$?
   always even   **always odd**   **could be even or odd**

15 Simplify   (a) $7x - 5x + 3x$,   (b) $a - 3b + 2a - b$,   (c) $3 \times m \times m$.

16 A sequence begins: 1, 2, 6, 16, …
   This is the rule continuing the sequence.

ADD THE PREVIOUS TWO NUMBERS TOGETHER AND THEN MULTIPLY BY TWO

   Deepak says the next term in the sequence is 22. Is he correct? **Explain your answer.**   AQA

17 This conversion graph can be used to
   change euros to dollars.

   (a) Use the graph to find
       (i) 20 euros in dollars,
       (ii) 30 dollars in euros.

   (b) Explain how you can use the graph
       to change 100 euros into dollars.

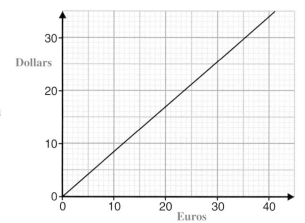

18 Solve these equations.
   (a) $g - 5 = 3$ (b) $4 + a = 9$ (c) $7x = 42$ (d) $5x + 4 = 19$

19 Umbrellas cost £4 each.
   (a) Write a formula for the cost, C, in pounds, of u umbrellas.
   (b) Find the value of u when $C = 28$.

20 (a) Copy and complete the table of values for the
       equation $y = x - 2$.

x	−1	1	3
y		−1	

   (b) Draw the graph of $y = x - 2$ for values of x from −1 to 3.
   (c) What are the coordinates of the points where the graph crosses the x axis and the y axis?

21 A large envelope costs x pence and a small envelope costs y pence.
   Write an expression for the cost of 3 large envelopes and 5 small envelopes.

22 (a) Find the value of $3m - 5$ when $m = 4$.
   (b) $T = 3m - 5$. Find the value of m when $T = 4$.
   (c) $P = 5y^2$. Find the value of P when $y = 3$.

23 Jaspel says to his friends:

"Think of a number, add 5, then divide by 2. Tell me your answer."

   (a) Huw thinks of the number 7. What is his answer?
   (b) Gary says his answer is 11. What number did he start with?   AQA

24 (a) What is the reciprocal of 0.25?

(b) Calculate $2.5^2 + \dfrac{1}{2.5}$.

25 Here is a rule for working out a sequence of numbers.

| Choose a starting number S | ▶ | Multiply by 3 | ▶ | Subtract 4 | ▶ | Write down the final number F. |

Write down an **equation** connecting the final number, F, and the starting number, S. AQA

26 (a) Draw the line $y = 2x + 1$ for values of x from -1 to 2.

(b) The line $y = 2x + 1$ crosses the line $x = -5$ at P.
Give the coordinates of P.

27 Solve these equations.

(a) $2x + 6 = 14$ (b) $3g - 5 = 4$ (c) $10y = 5$ (d) $6 + 2y = 4$

28 I think of a number. If I double my number and add 1, my answer is 35.

(a) Write down an equation to describe this.

(b) What number am I thinking of? AQA

29 The graph shows the journey of a cyclist from Halton to Kendal.
The distance from Halton to Kendal is 30 miles.

(a) For how long did the cyclist stop
during the journey?

(b) What was the average speed for
the part of the journey from A to B?

(c) On which section of the journey was
the cyclist travelling at his fastest speed?
Explain clearly how you got your answer.

(d) The cyclist stayed in Kendal for 2 hours.
He then returned to Halton, without stopping,
at an average speed of 12 miles per hour.
Calculate the time he arrived back in Halton.

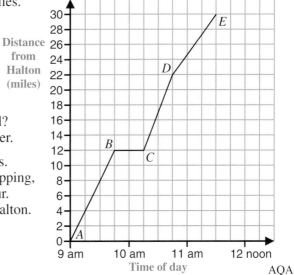

AQA

30 (a) Solve the equations (i) $4(a - 2) = 6$, (ii) $5t + 3 = -1 + t$.

(b) The sum of the numbers x, $x - 3$ and $x + 7$ is 25.
By forming an equation in x, find the value of x.

31 (a) Simplify $3n - n + 5$.

(b) Work out the value of $2x + y^3$ when $x = -3$ and $y = 2$. AQA

32 (a) Factorise (i) $3a - 6$, (ii) $k^2 - 2k$.

(b) Multiply out (i) $5(x + 3)$, (ii) $m(m - 4)$.

(c) Solve (i) $3 - 4x = x + 8$, (ii) $3(2x + 1) = 6$.

33 (a) Use your calculator to find $3.5^3 + \sqrt{18.4}$. Give all the figures on your calculator.

(b) Write your answer to 1 significant figure. AQA

34 A pencil costs x pence. A crayon costs $x + 3$ pence.

(a) Write an expression in terms of x for the cost of 5 crayons.

One pencil and 5 crayons cost 87 pence.

(b) By forming an equation in x, find the cost of the pencil. AQA

What you need to know

- You should be able to use a **protractor** to measure and draw angles accurately.

Eg 1 Measure the size of this angle.

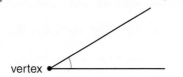

vertex ●

The angle measures 30°.

To measure an angle, the protractor is placed so that its centre point is on the corner (vertex) of the angle, with the base along one of the arms of the angle, as shown.

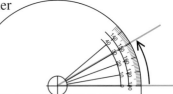

- Types and names of angles.

Acute angle	**Right angle**	**Obtuse angle**	**Reflex angle**
$0° < a < 90°$	$a = 90°$	$90° < a < 180°$	$180° < a < 360°$

- Angle properties.

Angles at a point	**Complementary angles**	**Supplementary angles**	**Vertically opposite angles**
	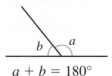	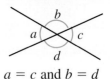	
$a + b + c = 360°$	$x + y = 90°$	$a + b = 180°$	$a = c$ and $b = d$

- Lines which meet at right angles are **perpendicular** to each other.

- A straight line joining two points is called a **line segment**.

- Lines which never meet and are always the same distance apart are **parallel**.

- When two parallel lines are crossed by a **transversal** the following pairs of angles are formed.

Corresponding angles — $a = c$

Alternate angles — $b = c$

Allied angles — $b + d = 180°$

Arrowheads are used to show that lines are **parallel**.

- You should be able to use angle properties to solve problems involving lines and angles.

Eg 2 Work out the size of the angles marked with letters.
Give a reason for each answer.

$a + 64° = 180°$ (supplementary angles)
$a = 180° - 64° = 116°$

$b = 64°$ (vertically opposite angles)
$c = 64°$ (corresponding angles)

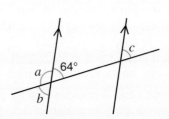

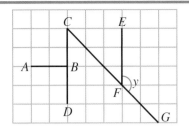

1 Look at the diagram.

   (a) Which lines are parallel to each other?
   (b) Which lines are perpendicular to each other?
   (c) (i) Measure angle y.
        (ii) Which of these words describes angle y?

       acute angle   **obtuse angle**   **reflex angle**

2 This shape contains a right angle, acute angles, obtuse angles and a reflex angle.

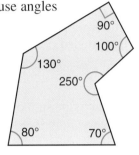

Write down the size of
   (a) one of the acute angles,
   (b) one of the obtuse angles,
   (c) the reflex angle.

AQA

3 Without measuring, find the size of the lettered angles.
Give a reason for each of your answers.

  (a)   (b)   (c)

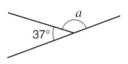 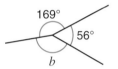 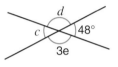

4

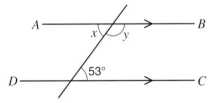

AB is parallel to *DC*.

   (a) Work out the size of angle x.
        Give a reason for your answer.
   (b) Work out the size of angle y.
        Give a reason for your answer.

5 In the diagram, the lines *PQ* and *RS* are parallel.

   (a) What is the size of angle x?
        Give a reason for your answer.
   (b) Find the size of angle y.

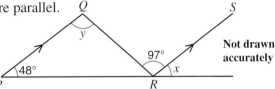

Not drawn accurately

AQA

6

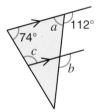

Work out the size of the angles marked with letters.
Give a reason for each answer.

7 Find the size of the angles marked with letters.

  (a)   (b)   (c)

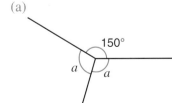 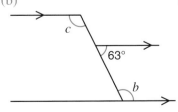 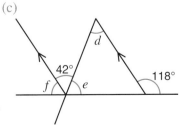

Triangles

What you need to know

- A **triangle** is a shape made by three straight sides.

- Triangles can be: **acute-angled** (all angles less than 90°),
  obtuse-angled (one angle greater than 90°),
  right-angled (one angle equal to 90°).

- The sum of the angles in a triangle is 180°.
  $$a + b + c = 180°$$

- The exterior angle is equal to the sum of the two opposite interior angles. $a + b = d$

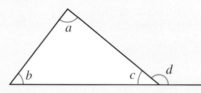

- Types of triangle:

  Scalene   **Isosceles**   **Equilateral**

 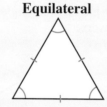

> A **sketch** is used when an accurate drawing is not required. Dashes across lines show sides that are equal in length. Equal angles are marked using arcs.

- You should be able to use properties of triangles to solve problems.

  Eg 1 Find the size of the angles marked a and b.

  $a = 86° + 51°$ (ext. ∠ of a Δ)
  $a = 137°$
  $b + 137° = 180°$ (supp. ∠'s)
  $b = 43°$

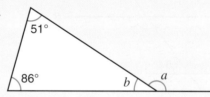

- Perimeter of a triangle is the sum of its three sides.

- Area of a triangle $= \dfrac{\text{base} \times \text{perpendicular height}}{2}$

  $$A = \frac{1}{2} \times b \times h$$

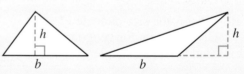

  Eg 2 Calculate the area of this triangle.

  $A = \dfrac{1}{2} \times b \times h$

  $= \dfrac{1}{2} \times 9 \times 6 \, \text{cm}^2$

  $= 27 \, \text{cm}^2$

  6 cm

  9 cm

- You should be able to draw triangles accurately, using ruler, compasses and protractor.

Exercise 26

1 Without measuring, work out the size of the angles marked with letters.

(a)
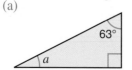
63°
a

(b)
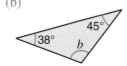
45°
38°
b

(c)
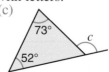
73°
c
52°

2 In the diagram, *ABX* is a straight line.
Work out the size of angle *ACB*.

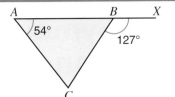

AQA

3
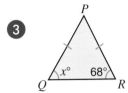

The diagram shows triangle *PQR*, with *PQ* = *PR*.
Work out the value of *x*.
Give a reason for your answer.

AQA

4 The diagram shows an isosceles triangle with two sides extended.
(a) Work out the size of angle *x*.
(b) Work out the size of angle *y*.

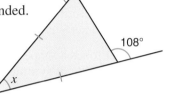

AQA

5
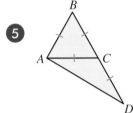

In the diagram *AB* = *BC* = *CA* = *CD*.
Work out the size of angle *CDA*.
Explain how you found your answer.

AQA

6 Make accurate drawings of these triangles using the information given.

(a)
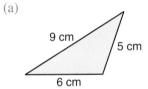

(b)
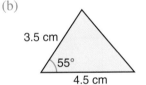

(c)
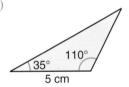

7 Find the areas of these triangles.

(a) (b)
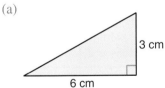

(c)

8 (a) Construct accurately a triangle with sides of 8 cm, 6 cm and 5 cm.
(b) By measuring the base and height, calculate the area of the triangle.

9 The diagram shows triangle *PQR*.
Calculate the area of triangle *PQR*.

AQA

10
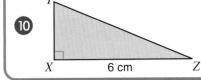

Triangle *XYZ* has an area of 12 cm².
XZ = 6 cm.
Calculate *YX*.

Triangles . . . Triangles . . . Triangles . . . Triangles . . .

Symmetry and Congruence

- A two-dimensional shape has **line symmetry** if the line divides the shape so that one side fits exactly over the other.

- A two-dimensional shape has **rotational symmetry** if it fits into a copy of its outline as it is rotated through 360°.

- A shape is only described as having rotational symmetry if the order of rotational symmetry is 2 or more.

- The number of times a shape fits into its outline in a single turn is the **order of rotational symmetry**.

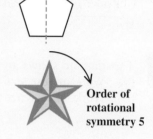

Order of rotational symmetry 5

Eg 1 For each of these shapes (a) draw and state the number of lines of symmetry,
 (b) state the order of rotational symmetry.

(i) 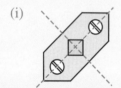 (ii) 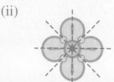 (iii)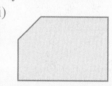

Two lines of symmetry.
Rotational symmetry of order 2.

4 lines of symmetry.
Order of rotational symmetry 4.

No lines of symmetry.
Order of rotational symmetry 1.
The shape is **not** described as having rotational symmetry.

- A **plane of symmetry** slices through a three-dimensional object so that one half is the mirror image of the other half.

- Three-dimensional objects can have **axes of symmetry**.

Eg 2 Sketch a cuboid and show its axes of symmetry.

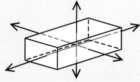

A cuboid has three axes of symmetry. The order of rotational symmetry about each axis is 2.

- When two shapes are the same shape and size they are said to be **congruent**.

- There are four ways to show that a pair of triangles are congruent.

SSS 3 corresponding sides.	**ASA** 2 angles and a corresponding side.
SAS 2 sides and the included angle.	**RHS** Right angle, hypotenuse and one other side.

Eg 3 Which of these triangles are congruent to each other? Give a reason for your answer.

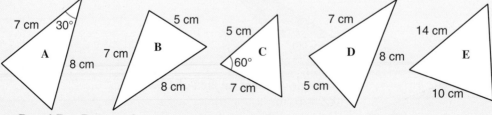

B and D.   Reason: 3 corresponding sides (SSS)

1 Half of a shape is drawn on squared paper, as shown.
AB is a line of symmetry for the complete shape.
Copy the diagram and complete the shape.

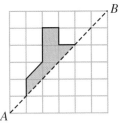

2 Consider the letters of the word ⠀⠀**O R A N G E**

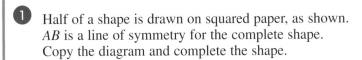

Which letters have ⠀(a)⠀ line symmetry only,
⠀⠀⠀⠀⠀⠀⠀⠀⠀⠀⠀(b)⠀ rotational symmetry only,
⠀⠀⠀⠀⠀⠀⠀⠀⠀⠀⠀(c)⠀ line symmetry and rotational symmetry?

3 For each of these shapes state ⠀(i)⠀ the number of lines of symmetry,
⠀⠀⠀⠀⠀⠀⠀⠀⠀⠀⠀⠀⠀⠀⠀⠀⠀⠀⠀⠀(ii)⠀ the order of rotational symmetry.

⠀(a) ⠀⠀⠀⠀⠀⠀⠀⠀(b) ⠀⠀⠀⠀⠀⠀⠀⠀(c) ⠀⠀⠀⠀⠀⠀⠀⠀(d)

  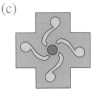

4 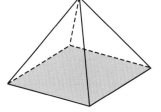 The diagram shows part of a shape.
Complete the shape so that it has
rotational symmetry of order 2.

AQA

5 The diagram shows a square-based pyramid.
⠀(a)⠀ How many planes of symmetry has the pyramid?
⠀(b)⠀ How many axes of symmetry has the pyramid?

6 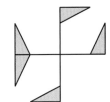 The diagram shows a rectangle which has been cut into 6 pieces.
Which two pieces are congruent to each other?

7 ⠀(a)⠀ Complete this shape so that it has both line symmetry
⠀⠀⠀⠀ and rotational symmetry.

⠀(b)⠀ Which of these triangles are congruent to each other?
⠀⠀⠀⠀ Give a reason for your answer.

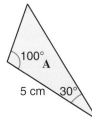 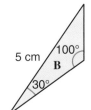 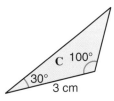 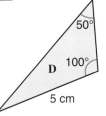

AQA

Symmetry and Congruence

Quadrilaterals

What you need to know

- A **quadrilateral** is a shape made by four straight lines.

- The sum of the angles in a quadrilateral is 360°.

- The **perimeter** of a quadrilateral is the sum of the lengths of its four sides.

$$a + b + c + d = 360°$$

- Facts about these special quadrilaterals:

parallelogram   rectangle   square   rhombus   trapezium   isosceles trapezium   kite

Quadrilateral	Sides	Angles	Diagonals	Line symmetry	Order of rotational symmetry	Area formula
Parallelogram	Opposite sides equal and parallel	Opposite angles equal	Bisect each other	0	2	$A = bh$
Rectangle	Opposite sides equal and parallel	All 90°	Bisect each other	2	2	$A = bh$
Rhombus	4 equal sides, opposite sides parallel	Opposite angles equal	Bisect each other at 90°	2	2	$A = bh$
Square	4 equal sides, opposite sides parallel	All 90°	Bisect each other at 90°	4	4	$A = l^2$
Trapezium	1 pair of parallel sides					$A = \frac{1}{2}(a + b)h$
Isosceles trapezium	1 pair of parallel sides, non-parallel sides equal	2 pairs of equal angles	Equal in length	1	1*	$A = \frac{1}{2}(a + b)h$
Kite	2 pairs of adjacent sides equal	1 pair of opposite angles equal	One bisects the other at 90°	1	1*	

*A shape is only described as having rotational symmetry if the order of rotational symmetry is 2 or more.

- You should be able to use properties of quadrilaterals to solve problems.

Eg 1 Work out the size of the angle marked x.

Opposite angles are equal.
So, $125° + 125° + x + x = 360°$
$x = 55°$

Eg 2 Find the area of this trapezium.

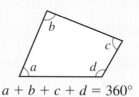

$A = \frac{1}{2}(a + b)h$

$= \frac{1}{2}(6 + 9)5$

$= \frac{1}{2} \times 15 \times 5$

$= 37.5 \, cm^2$

- You should be able to construct a quadrilateral from given information using ruler, protractor, compasses.

1 This rectangle is drawn on 1 cm squared paper.
It has a perimeter of 18 cm.
  (a) What is the area of the rectangle?
  (b) (i) On 1 cm squared paper draw three different
          rectangles which each have a perimeter of 18 cm.
      (ii) Find the area of each rectangle.

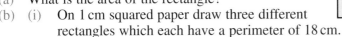 **Not full size**

2 A quadrilateral with 4 equal sides and 4 right angles is called a square.
What is the mathematical name given to:
  (a) A quadrilateral with 4 equal sides but no right angles?
  (b) A quadrilateral with 2 pairs of opposite sides equal but diagonals of different lengths?
  (c) A quadrilateral with only 1 pair of parallel sides of unequal lengths?   AQA

3 Find the size of the lettered angles.
  (a)   (b)   (c)

 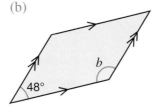 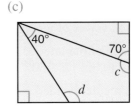

4 The diagram shows a quadrilateral $ABCD$.
$AB = BC$ and $CD = DA$.
  (a) Which of the following correctly describes the quadrilateral $ABCD$?

      rhombus   **parallelogram**   **kite**   **trapezium**

  (b) Angle $ADC = 36°$ and angle $BCD = 105°$.
      Work out the size of angle ABC.

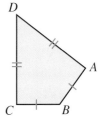

5 A rectangle is 4 cm wide and 9 cm long.
What is the length of the side of a square with exactly the same area?

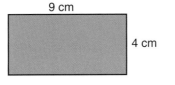

                                           AQA

6 A rectangle measures 8.6 cm by 6.4 cm.
  (a) Find the perimeter of the rectangle.   (b) Find the area of the rectangle.

7 Two triangles are joined together to form a rhombus as shown.
The perimeter of the rhombus is 36 cm.
The perimeter of each triangle is 24 cm.
Find the value of b.

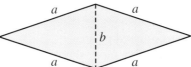

                                           AQA

8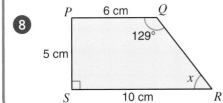

The diagram shows a trapezium $PQRS$.

  (a) Work out the size of the angle marked x.

  (b) Calculate the area of the trapezium.

What you need to know

- A **polygon** is a many-sided shape made by straight lines.

- A polygon with all sides equal and all angles equal is called a **regular polygon**.

- Shapes you need to know: A 3-sided polygon is called a **triangle**.
  A 4-sided polygon is called a **quadrilateral**.
  A 5-sided polygon is called a **pentagon**.
  A 6-sided polygon is called a **hexagon**.

- The sum of the exterior angles of any polygon is 360°.

- At each vertex of a polygon: interior angle + exterior angle = 180°

- The sum of the interior angles of an n-sided polygon is given by:
  $(n - 2) \times 180°$

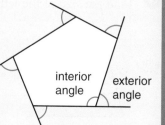

interior angle   exterior angle

- For a regular n-sided polygon: exterior angle $= \dfrac{360°}{n}$

- You should be able to use the properties of polygons to solve problems.

Eg 1   Find the sum of the interior angles of a pentagon.
$(5 - 2) \times 180° = 3 \times 180° = 540°$

> A pentagon has 5 sides, so substitute
> $n = 5$ into $(n - 2) \times 180°$.

Eg 2   A regular polygon has an exterior angle of 30°.
(a)   How many sides has the polygon?
(b)   What is the size of an interior angle of the polygon?

(a) $n = \dfrac{360°}{\text{exterior angle}}$

$n = \dfrac{360°}{30°}$

$n = 12$

(b)   int. ∠ + ext. ∠ = 180°
int. ∠ + 30° = 180°
interior angle = 150°

- A shape will **tessellate** if it covers a surface without overlapping and leaves no gaps.

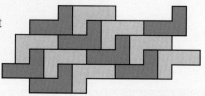

- All triangles tessellate.

- All quadrilaterals tessellate.

- Equilateral triangles, squares and hexagons can be used to make **regular tessellations**.

Exercise 29

1   Copy the shape onto squared paper.
On your diagram, draw **five** more shapes to show how the shape tessellates.

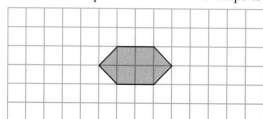

AQA

2 These shapes are drawn on isometric paper.

What are the differences between the symmetry of shape *A* and the symmetry of shape *B*?

3 Work out the size of the angles marked with letters.

(a)

75°   127°   *a*

(b)

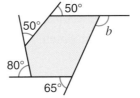

(c)

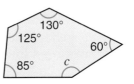

4 These shapes are regular polygons. Work out the size of the lettered angles.

(a)

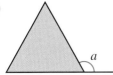

(b)

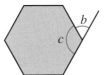

(c)

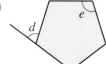

5 The diagram shows part of a regular polygon.
The exterior angles of this polygon are 24°.
How many sides has the polygon?

6 Four regular pentagons are placed together, as shown, to form a rhombus, *ABCD*.

Calculate the size of
(a)   angle *ABC*,
(b)   angle *XCY*.

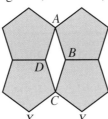

7

The diagram shows a hexagon.
Show that the sum of the interior angles of a hexagon is 720°.

8 (a)   Here is a tessellation of regular hexagons and equilateral triangles.
Explain why these shapes fit together exactly at point *P*.

(b)   Draw a tessellation which uses squares and regular octagons.

(c)   Explain clearly why regular octagons will **not** tessellate with
equilateral triangles.
(You may wish to use sketches to illustrate your answer.)

(d)   A different regular polygon will tessellate with
equilateral triangles.
Here is a sketch of part of the tessellation.
How many sides must the regular polygon have?
Show your working.

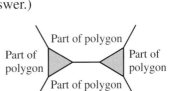

AQA

Direction and Distance

What you need to know

- **Compass points**

  The angle between North and East is 90°.
  The angle between North and North-East is 45°.

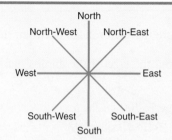

- **Bearings** are used to describe the direction in which you must travel to get from one place to another.

- A bearing is an angle measured from the North line in a clockwise direction.
  A bearing can be any angle from 0° to 360° and is written as a three-figure number.

  To find a bearing:
      measure angle *a* to find the bearing of *Y* from *X*,
      measure angle *b* to find the bearing of *X* from *Y*.

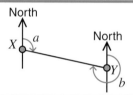

- You should be able to use **scales** and **bearings** to interpret and draw accurate diagrams.

  There are two ways to describe a scale.
  1. A scale of 1 cm to 10 km means that a distance of 1 cm on the map represents an actual distance of 10 km.
  2. A scale of 1 : 10 000 means that all distances measured on the map have to be multiplied by 10 000 to find the real distance.

Eg 1 The diagram shows the plan of a stage in a car rally.
The plan has been drawn to a scale of 1 : 50 000.

  (a) What is the bearing of *Q* from *P*?
  (b) What is the bearing of *P* from *R*?
  (c) What is the actual distance from *P* to *R* in metres?

  (a) 080°
  (b) 295°
  (c) 3500 m

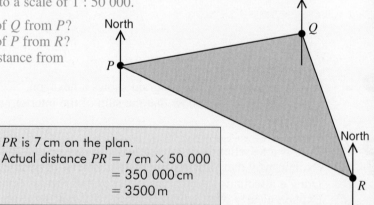

PR is 7 cm on the plan.
Actual distance *PR* = 7 cm × 50 000
                     = 350 000 cm
                     = 3500 m

Exercise 30

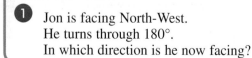

1 Jon is facing North-West.
He turns through 180°.
In which direction is he now facing?

2 This is a map of Scotland with five towns marked.

(a) Which town is South-West of Aberdeen?

(b) Write the direction South-West as a 3-figure bearing.

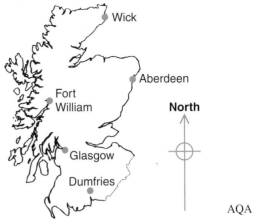

3 A bridge is 2600 m in length.
A plan of the bridge has been drawn to a scale of 1 cm to 100 m.
What is the length of the bridge on the plan?

4

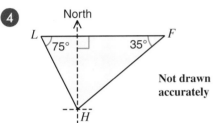

Not drawn accurately

A fishing boat sails from a harbour, *H*, to a point, *F*.
F is due East of a lighthouse, *L*.
Angle *FLH* is 75° and angle *LFH* is 35°.

(a) Calculate the bearing of *F* from *H*.
(b) Calculate the bearing of *L* from *H*.
(c) Calculate the bearing of *H* from *F*.

5 The map shows the position of a ship, *P*, and a lighthouse, *L*.

(a) What is the bearing of *P* from *L*?

Copy the diagram onto one-centimetre squared paper.

(b) Another ship, *Q*, is due North of *L*.
Q is on a bearing of 055° from *P*.
Mark clearly the position of *Q* on your diagram.

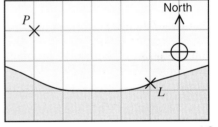

6

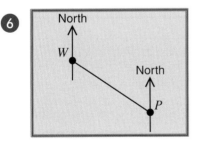

The map shows the positions of a windmill, *W*, and a pylon, *P*.

(a) What is the bearing of
(i) the pylon from the windmill,
(ii) the windmill from the pylon?

The map has been drawn to a scale of 2 cm to 5 km.

(b) Use the map to find the distance *WP* in kilometres.

7 The diagram shows a sketch of the course to be used for a running event.

(a) Draw an accurate plan of the course, using a scale of 1 cm to represent 100 m.

(b) Use your plan to find
(i) the bearing of *X* from *Y*,
(ii) the distance *XY* in metres.

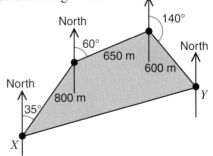

Circles

●●●●●●●●●●●●●●●●●●●

What you need to know

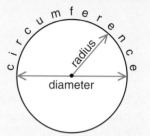

- A **circle** is the shape drawn by keeping a pencil the same distance from a fixed point on a piece of paper.

- The meaning of the following words:
  Circumference – special name used for the perimeter of a circle.

  Radius – distance from the centre of a circle to any point on the circumference.
  The plural of radius is **radii**.

  Diameter – distance right across the circle, passing through the centre point. The diameter is twice as long as the radius.

  Chord – a line joining two points on the circumference. The longest chord is the diameter.

  Tangent – a line which touches the circumference of a circle at one point only.

  Arc – part of the circumference of a circle.

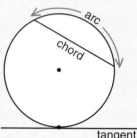

- The **circumference** of a circle is given by: $\boxed{C = \pi \times d \ \text{ or } \ C = 2 \times \pi \times r}$

- The **area** of a circle is given by: $\boxed{A = \pi \times r^2}$

- You should be able to solve problems which involve finding the circumference or the area of a circle.

  Eg 1 A circle has a radius of 4 cm.
  Estimate: (a) the circumference of the circle,   (b) the area of the circle.

  (a) $C = 2 \times \pi \times r$ (b) $A = \pi \times r \times r$
  $\quad\;\; C = 2 \times 3 \times 4$ $\quad\;\; A = 3 \times 4 \times 4$ | When **estimating**, take π to be 3. |
  $\quad\;\; C = 24$ cm $\quad\;\; A = 48$ cm²

  | For more accurate calculations, take π to be 3.14 or use the π key on your calculator. |

  Eg 2 Calculate the circumference of a circle with diameter 18 cm.
  Give your answer to 1 d.p.

  $C = \pi \times d$
  $C = \pi \times 18$
  $C = 56.548...$
  $C = 56.5$ cm, correct to 1 d.p.

  Eg 3 Calculate the area of a circle with diameter 12 cm.
  Give your answer to the nearest whole number.

  $A = \pi \times r^2$
  $A = \pi \times 6 \times 6$ | $r = \dfrac{\text{diameter}}{2}$ |
  $A = 113.097...$
  $A = 113$ cm², to the nearest whole number.

Exercise 31

Do not use a calculator for question 1.

1 A coin has a diameter of 1.96 cm.
Estimate the circumference of the coin.

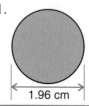

1.96 cm

AQA

Questions 2 to 10. Take π to be 3.14 or use the π key on your calculator.

2 A circular pond has a radius of 3 metres.
  (a) Calculate the circumference of the pond.
  (b) Calculate the area of the pond.   AQA

3 A circle has a diameter of 7 cm.
  (a) Calculate the circumference of this circle.
  (b) Calculate the area of this circle.   AQA

4 (a) Jayne has a circular hoop of radius 35 cm.
          Calculate the circumference of her hoop.
     (b) Jayne puts the hoop down on the ground.
          Calculate the area inside the hoop.   AQA

5   Tranter has completed three-fifths of a circular jigsaw puzzle.
          The puzzle has a radius of 20 cm.
          What area of the puzzle is complete?

6 Mr Kray's lawn is 25 m in length.
He rolls it with a garden roller.
The garden roller has a diameter of 0.4 m.
Work out the number of times the roller rotates when
rolling the length of the lawn once.

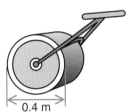

0.4 m

7  The top of a table is a circle with a radius of 55 cm.
          (a) Calculate the circumference of the table top.

          On the table are 6 place mats.
          Each place mat is a circle with a diameter of 18 cm.
          (b) What area of the table top is **not** covered by place mats?

8 Calculate the area of a circle with radius 4.3 cm.   AQA

9 Each wheel on Hannah's bicycle has a radius of 15 cm.
Calculate how many complete revolutions each wheel makes when Hannah cycles 100 metres.

10 Discs of card are used in the packaging of frozen pizzas.
Each disc fits the base of the pizza exactly.

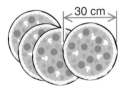

30 cm

  (a) Calculate the area of a disc used to pack a large pizza
       with a diameter of 30 cm.

  (b) The discs for large pizzas are cut from sheets of card 300 cm by 100 cm.

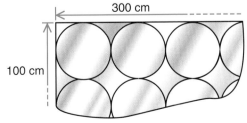

300 cm

100 cm

  (i)   How many discs can be cut from each sheet?
  (ii) What area of each sheet is wasted?

Area and Volume

What you need to know

- **Faces**, **vertices** (corners) and **edges**.

  A cube has 6 faces, 8 vertices and 12 edges.

  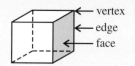

- A **net** can be used to make a solid shape.

  Eg 1 Draw a net of a cube.

- **Isometric paper** is used to make 2-dimensional drawings of 3-dimensional shapes.

  Eg 2 Draw a cube of edge 2 cm on isometric paper.

- **Plans and Elevations**

  The view of a 3-dimensional shape looking from above is called a **plan**.
  The view of a 3-dimensional shape from the front or sides is called an **elevation**.

  Eg 3 Draw diagrams to show the plan and elevation from **X**, for this 3-dimensional shape.

  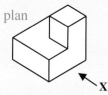
  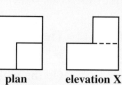

  plan   elevation X

  Dotted lines are used to show hidden edges.

- **Volume** is the amount of space occupied by a 3-dimensional shape.

- The formula for the volume of a **cuboid** is:
  Volume = length × breadth × height
  $V = l \times b \times h$

  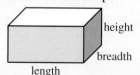

- Volume of a **cube** is: $V = l^3$

- To find the **surface area** of a cuboid, find the areas of the 6 rectangular faces and add the answers together.

  Eg 4 Find the volume and surface area of a cuboid measuring 7 cm by 5 cm by 3 cm.

  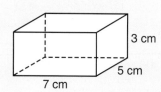

  $$\text{Volume} = l \times b \times h$$
  $$= 7\,\text{cm} \times 5\,\text{cm} \times 3\,\text{cm}$$
  $$= 105\,\text{cm}^3$$

  $$\text{Surface area} = (2 \times 7 \times 5) + (2 \times 5 \times 3) + (2 \times 3 \times 7)$$
  $$= 70 + 30 + 42$$
  $$= 142\,\text{cm}^2$$

- Shapes formed by joining different shapes together are called **compound shapes**.
  To find the area of a compound shape we must first split the shape up into rectangles, squares and triangles. Find the area of each part and then add the answers together.

  Eg 5 Find the total area of this shape.

  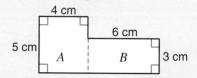

  Area $A = 5 \times 4 = 20\,\text{cm}^2$
  Area $B = 6 \times 3 = 18\,\text{cm}^2$
  Total area $= 20 + 18 = 38\,\text{cm}^2$

1 This shape is a pyramid.
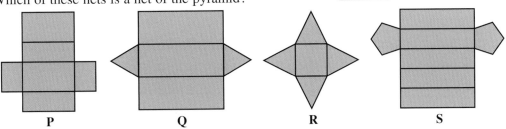

(a) How many faces, edges and vertices has the pyramid?

(b) Which of these nets is a net of the pyramid?

| P | Q | R | S |

2 The diagram shows a solid drawn on isometric paper.
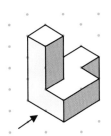

(a) Draw the plan of the solid.

(b) Draw the elevation of the solid from the direction shown by the arrow.

3

This shape has been drawn on 1 cm squared paper.

(a) Find the perimeter of the shape.

(b) Find the area of the shape.

(c) On 1 cm squared paper, draw a different shape with the same area.

AQA

Not full size

4 Find the area of this shape.
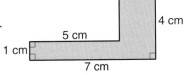

4 cm
5 cm
1 cm
7 cm

5 Identical blocks are used to make a base for a barbecue.
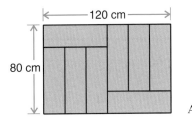

(a) Calculate the perimeter of the base.

(b) Calculate the length and the width of each block.

120 cm
80 cm

AQA

6
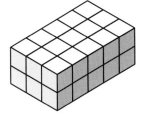

This cuboid has been made using cubes of side 1 cm.

(a) How many cubes are needed to make the cuboid?

(b) (i) Draw a net of the cuboid on 1 cm squared paper.
    (ii) Hence, find the surface area of the cuboid.

7 (a) Which of these cuboids has the larger volume?
Show all your working.
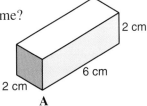
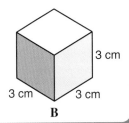

(b) Which cuboid has the larger surface area?

2 cm
6 cm
2 cm
A

3 cm
3 cm
3 cm
B

Transformations

What you need to know

- The movement of a shape from one position to another is called a **transformation**.
- **Single transformations** can be described in terms of a reflection, a rotation, a translation or an enlargement.
- **Reflection**: The image of the shape is the same distance from the mirror line as the original.
- **Rotation**: All points are turned through the same angle about the same point, called a centre of rotation.
- **Translation**: All points are moved the same distance in the same direction without turning.
- **Enlargement**: All lengths are multiplied by a scale factor.

$$\text{Scale factor} = \frac{\text{new length}}{\text{original length}}$$ | New length = scale factor × original length |

- You should be able to draw the transformation of a shape.

Eg 1 Draw the image of triangle P after it has been translated 3 units to the left and 2 units up.

  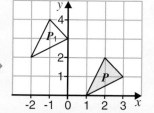

- You should be able to fully describe transformations.

Transformation	Image same shape and size?	Details needed to describe the transformation
Reflection	Yes	Mirror line, sometimes given as an equation.
Rotation	Yes	Centre of rotation, amount of turn, direction of turn.
Translation	Yes	Horizontal movement and vertical movement.
Enlargement	No	Centre of enlargement, scale factor.

Eg 2 Describe the single transformation which maps

  (a) A onto B,   (b) A onto C,   (c) A onto D,   (d) A onto E.

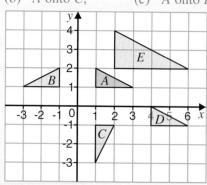

  (a) **Reflection** in the y axis.
  (b) **Rotation** of 90° clockwise about the origin.
  (c) **Translation** 3 units to the right and 2 units down.
  (d) **Enlargement** scale factor 2, centre (0, 0).

1 Copy each diagram and draw the transformation given.

(a) Reflect the shape in the *x* axis.

(b) Translate the shape, 2 units left and 3 units up.

(c) Rotate the shape, 90° clockwise about the origin.

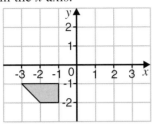 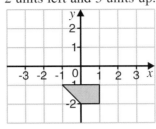 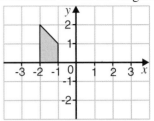

2 In each diagram *A* is mapped onto *B* by a single transformation. Describe each transformation.

(a)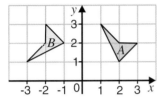

(b)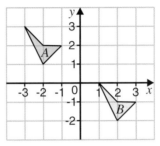

(c)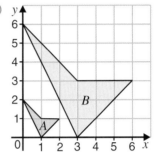

3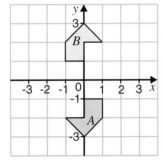

The diagram shows two positions of a shape. Describe fully the single transformation which takes *A* onto *B*.

AQA

4 Copy the diagram and draw the reflection of the shaded triangle in the *y* axis.

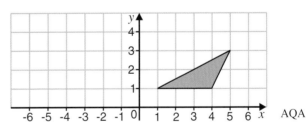

AQA

5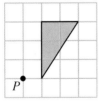

Copy the triangle onto squared paper and enlarge it by a scale factor of 4. Use the point marked *P* as the centre of enlargement.

AQA

6 The diagram shows the positions of kites *P*, *Q* and *R*.

(a) *P* is mapped onto *Q* by a reflection. What is the equation of the line of reflection?

(b) *P* is mapped onto *R* by a translation. Describe the translation.

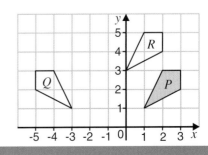

| SECTION 34 | **Understanding and Using Measures** |

What you need to know

- The common units — both **metric** and **imperial** — used to measure **length**, **mass** and **capacity**.

- How to estimate measurements using sensible units and a suitable degree of accuracy.

  Eg 1 You would use centimetres to measure the length of a pencil and give the answer to the nearest tenth of a centimetre.

- How to convert from one unit to another. This includes knowing the connection between one metric unit and another and the approximate equivalents between metric and imperial units.

Metric Units	**Imperial Units**	**Conversions**
Length 1 kilometre (km) = 1000 metres (m) 1 m = 100 centimetres (cm) 1 cm = 10 mm	**Length** 1 foot = 12 inches 1 yard = 3 feet	**Length** 5 miles is about 8 km 1 inch is about 2.5 cm 1 foot is about 30 cm
Mass 1 tonne (t) = 1000 kilograms (kg) 1 kg = 1000 grams (g)	**Mass** 1 pound = 16 ounces 14 pounds = 1 stone	**Mass** 1 kg is about 2.2 pounds
Capacity and volume 1 litre = 1000 millilitres (ml) 1 cm³ = 1 ml	**Capacity and volume** 1 gallon = 8 pints	**Capacity and volume** 1 litre is about 1.75 pints 1 gallon is about 4.5 litres

- How to change between units of area. For example $1 \text{ m}^2 = 10\,000 \text{ cm}^2$.

- How to change between units of volume. For example $1 \text{ m}^3 = 1\,000\,000 \text{ cm}^3$.

- You should be able to solve problems involving different units.

  Eg 2 A tank holds 6 gallons of water.
 How many litres is this? $6 \times 4.5 = 27$ litres

  Eg 3 A cuboid measures 1.5 m by 90 cm by 80 cm.
 Calculate the volume of the cuboid, in m³. $1.5 \times 0.9 \times 0.8 = 1.08 \text{ m}^3$

- Be able to read scales accurately.

  Eg 4 Part of a scale is shown.
 It measures weight in grams.
 What weight is shown by the arrow? The arrow shows 27 grams.

Exercise 34

Do not use a calculator for questions 1 to 6.

1 Write down the metric unit you would use to measure
  (a) the length of a train,
  (b) the weight of a small pot of jam,
  (c) the amount of milk produced by a herd of cows each day.

2 A bookcase is 140 cm in height and weighs 8.5 kg.
  (a) What is the height of the bookcase in metres?
  (b) What is the weight of the bookcase in grams?

3 A glass contains 250 ml of milk. What fraction of a litre is this?

4 What value is shown by the pointer on each of these diagrams?

(a)

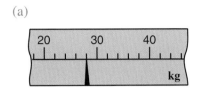

(b)

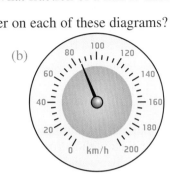

(c)

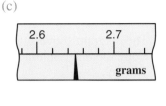

AQA

5 Write each of the following using a more suitable unit.
(a) The distance between two towns is 6000 metres.
(b) A mouse weighs 0.06 kilograms.
(c) A piece of paper has an area of 0.006 m².
(d) A room has a volume of 60 000 000 cm³.

6 Two villages are 40 km apart.
(a) Change 40 km into metres.
(b) How many miles are the same as 40 km? AQA

7 A rectangular doormat measures 150 cm by 120 cm.
Calculate the area of the doormat in square metres.

8 A tank holds 36 litres of oil. How many gallons is 36 litres?

9 Jemma has 3 litres of milk and 20 glasses. Each glass holds one third of a pint.
How many glasses can Jemma fill?

10 A chocolate cake is cut into 12 equal slices. Each slice weighs 3 ounces.
Given that 16 ounces = 1 pound, show that the whole cake weighs about 1 kg.

11 Serena measures the height of door A as 2 metres.
Tom measures the height of door B as 70 inches.
Which door is the higher, A or B? You must show all your working. AQA

12 Use the conversion │ 1 foot = 30.5 cm │ to change 28 feet into metres. AQA

13 │ One fluid ounce = 28.4 millilitres │
(a) Convert 8 fluid ounces to millimetres.

│ 1000 millilitres = 1 litre │

(b) Use your answer to (a) to explain why 8 fluid ounces is less than $\frac{1}{4}$ litre. AQA

14 Mum's Traditional Jam is sold in two sizes.
A 1 lb pot of jam costs 71 pence. A 1 kg pot of jam costs £1.50.
Which pot of jam is better value for money? You must show all your working.

15 Debbie is 5 feet 4 inches tall and weighs 9 stone 2 lb. Joyce is 155 cm tall and weighs 60 kg.
Who is taller? Who is heavier? You must show your working.

16 Last year Felicity drove 2760 miles on business.
Her car does 38 miles per gallon. Petrol costs 69 pence per litre.
She is given a car allowance of 25 pence per kilometre.
How much of her car allowance is left after paying for her petrol?
Give your answer to the nearest £.

Section Review – Shape, Space and Measures

The diagrams in this exercise have not been drawn accurately.

1 The diagram shows a line, *AB*, and a point, *C*.
Copy the diagram onto 1 cm squared paper.

   (a) Measure the length of the line *AB* in centimetres.
   (b) Mark the midpoint of the line *AB* with a cross.
   (c) Draw the line through *C* which is parallel to the line *AB*.

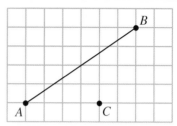

Not full size

AQA

2 The diagram shows some 3-dimensional shapes.

   (a) How many edges has shape *A*?
   (b) How many faces has shape *B*?
   (c) What is the mathematical name for shape *C*?

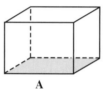

        A   **B**   **C**

3 (a)

The shape has been drawn on 1 cm squared paper.
What is the area of the shape?

Not full size

   (b) This solid has been made using 1 cm cubes.
      (i) What is the volume of the solid?
      (ii) Draw the plan of the solid.
      (iii) Draw the elevation of the solid from the direction shown by the arrow.

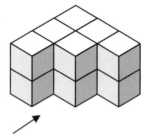

4

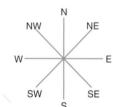

   (a) What fraction of a complete turn is it from South to North-West?

   (b) Isobel is facing East.
      She makes a $\frac{1}{4}$ turn anticlockwise.
      In which direction is she now facing?

5 (a) Which of these weights are the same?
      8000 g   80 kg   800 g   8 kg   0.08 kg

   (b) Which of these lengths is the longest?
      0.2 km   20 m   2000 mm   200 cm

   (c) The scales show weights in kilograms.
      Write down the weight of the pears.

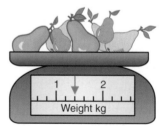

6 (a) Draw a circle of radius 5 cm.
   (b) Draw a diameter on your circle. Label its ends *A* and *B*.
   (c) Mark a point, *P*, anywhere on the circumference of your circle.
      Join *A* to *P* and *P* to *B*.
   (d) Use your protractor to measure the angle *APB*.

AQA

7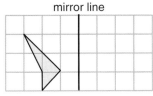

mirror line

Copy the diagram.
Draw the reflection of the shape in the mirror line.

8 (a) Use your protractor to measure the size of angles *x* and *y*.

(b) Which of these angles is an obtuse angle?

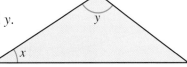

9

The diagram shows a circle with three equal segments shaded.
The diagram has rotational symmetry.
What is the order of rotational symmetry?

AQA

10 Seven shapes are shown.
Each square on the grid has sides 1 cm long.

(a) What is the perimeter of shape *C*?

(b) Which shape is congruent to shape *A*?

(c) On 1 cm squared paper show how
shapes *B* and *F* may be used to make
a rectangle with an area of 15 cm².
You may use more than one of each shape.

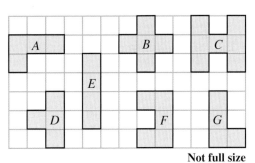

Not full size

AQA

11 Find the angles marked with letters. Give a reason for each of your answers.

(a)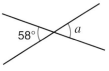

(b)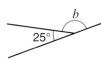

(c)

12 The diagram shows points *A*, *B* and *C*.

(a) What are the coordinates of *A*?

(b) What are the coordinates of *C*?

(c) *ABCD* is a square.
What are the coordinates of *D*?

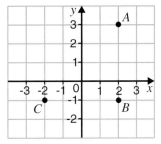

13 (a)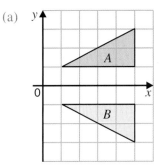

Describe the transformation which takes
triangle *A* onto triangle *B*.

(b) *AFGHI* is an enlargement
of the shaded shape *ABCDE*.
(i) What is the scale factor
of the enlargement?
(ii) Write down two lines
which are parallel.

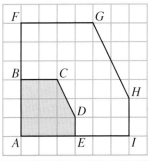

AQA

14 A jar contains 400 grams of marmalade. Peter buys 12 jars of marmalade.
   (a)   How much marmalade, in total, is there in these 12 jars? Give your answer in kilograms.
   (b)   Does this total amount of marmalade weigh more or less than ten pounds?
         You **must** show your working.
                                                                                    AQA

15 Find the size of the angles *a*, *b* and *c*.   Give a reason for each of your answers.
   (a)   (b)   (c)

16 The descriptions of two different quadrilaterals are given in the boxes below.
   Choose the correct names from this list.

   kite   rectangle   rhombus   square   trapezium

   (a)   One pair of sides are parallel but they are not equal in length.

   (b)   The diagonals are of different lengths and cross at 90°.
         Each diagonal is a line of symmetry of the quadrilateral.
                                                                                    AQA

17   (a)   Copy the diagram.
                 Shade two more squares so that the final diagram has line symmetry only.
           (b)   Make another copy of the diagram.
                 Shade two more squares so that the final diagram
                 has rotational symmetry only.

18 Part of a tessellation of triangles is shown.
   Copy the diagram onto squared paper.
   Continue the tessellation by drawing four more triangles.

19 Work out the area of each shape.
   (a)   (b)

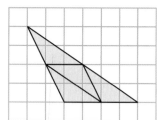

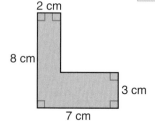

20   Copy the diagram onto squared paper.
           Draw an enlargement of the kite, scale factor 2, centre *X*.
                                                                                    AQA

21 (a)   A cuboid measures 2 cm by 2.5 cm by 4 cm.
              (i)   Draw an accurate net of the cuboid.
              (ii)   Calculate the total surface area of the cuboid.
        (b)   Another cuboid has a volume of 50 cm³. The base of the cuboid measures 4 cm by 5 cm.
              Calculate the height of the cuboid.

22 Colin is 5 feet 10 inches tall and weighs 11 stones.
   On a medical form he is asked to give his height in centimetres and his weight in kilograms.
   What values should he give?

23

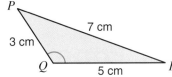

The diagram shows a sketch of a triangle.
By making an accurate drawing of the triangle,
find the size of angle *PQR*.

24 The diagram shows the positions of shapes *P*, *Q* and *R*.

(a) Describe the single transformation which takes *P* onto *Q*.

(b) Describe the single transformation which takes *P* onto *R*.

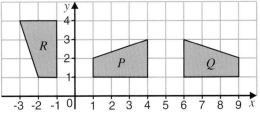

Copy shape *P* onto squared paper.
(c) *P* is translated 3 units to the left and 2 units up.
  (i) Draw the new position of *P* on your diagram. Label it *S*.
  (ii) Describe the translation which takes *S* back onto *P*.

25 Find the size of the angles *a*, *b*, *c* and *d*.

(a)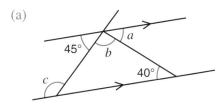

(b)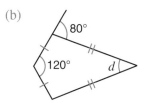

26 Sheila lives 6 kilometres from the beach.
She jogs from her home to the beach at an average speed of 10 km/h.
She gets to the beach at 1000.
Calculate the time when she left home.

AQA

27 The diagram shows the angle formed when three regular polygons are placed together, as shown.

(a) Explain why angle *a* is 120°.

(b) Work out the size of the angle marked *b*.

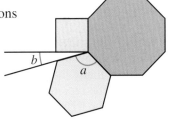

28 On a map the distance between two hospitals is 14.5 cm.
The map has been drawn to a scale of 1 to 250 000.
Calculate the actual distance between the hospitals in kilometres.

29

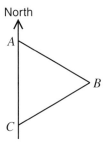

The sketch shows the positions of three footpaths which meet at *A*, *B* and *C*.
A is due north of *C*.
Triangle *ABC* is equilateral.

(a) Write down the three-figure bearing of *B* from *C*.

(b) Write down the three-figure bearing of *A* from *B*.

AQA

30 A circle of radius 5 cm is cut into quarters.
The quarters are put together to make shape *S*, as shown.

(a) Calculate the area of the shape *S*.

(b) Calculate the perimeter of shape *S*.

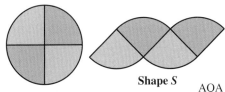

Shape *S*
AQA

81

Do not use a calculator for this exercise.

1 Bananas cost 89p per kilogram.
- (a) (i) How much do 3 kg of bananas cost?
  - (ii) Jane buys 3 kg of bananas and pays with a £5 note.
    How much change should she get?

BANANAS
89p
per kilogram

- (b) Barry also bought some bananas.
  The weight of bananas he bought is shown on the scales.
  What weight of bananas did Barry buy?
- (c) Michael bought 3.5 kg of bananas.
  How many grams is this?

AQA

2 Use these numbers to answer the following questions.

3	4	13	27	35	64

- (a) Which number is a factor of 16?
- (b) Which number is a multiple of 9?
- (c) Which two numbers add up to 40?

3 (a) A sequence uses this rule: | Add 3 to the last term. |

What term comes before 15 in this sequence?
- (b) Another sequence begins: 1, 2, 4, 8, 16, …
  - (i) What is the next term in this sequence?
  - (ii) Describe the rule you used to find the next term.

4 The diagram shows a rectangle and a triangle
drawn on 1 cm squared paper.
- (a) How many lines of symmetry has
  - (i) the rectangle,
  - (ii) the triangle?
- (b) What is the perimeter of the rectangle?
- (c) What is the area of the triangle?

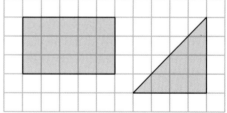

Not full size

5 (a) A ball costs x pence. How much will 3 balls cost?
- (b) A skipping rope costs 30 pence more than a ball. How much does a skipping rope cost?

6 Clare makes a solid shape by joining together cubes of side 1 cm.
- (a) Work out the volume of the solid.
- (b) Before she made the solid, she had 30 cubes.
  What fraction of the cubes did she use?

AQA

7 Use the formula $P = 5m + 2n$ to find the value of P when $m = 4$ and $n = 3$.

8 (a) Draw accurately triangle PQR in which $QP = 5$ cm, $PR = 8$ cm and angle $QPR = 45°$.
- (b) Measure the length of QR on your diagram.
- (c) Measure the size of angle QRP on your diagram.

9 (a) On graph paper plot the points $P(4, 1)$ and $Q(2, -5)$.
- (b) Find the coordinates of the midpoint of the line segment PQ.